FISHERS OF MEN

Becoming a Dynamic Disciple
of Jesus Christ

SHARON DUTRA

FISHERS OF MEN
Becoming a Dynamic Disciple of Jesus Christ

By Sharon Dutra

Printed in the United States of America

ISBN 978-0-578-67397-4

Cover Photo istock
Cover Design and Interior Layout by Bogdan Matei at UpWork.com

OTHER BOOKS BY THIS AUTHOR

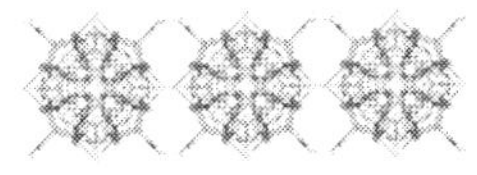

Be Transformed: By the Spirit of the Living God 2011 (Also available in Spanish and Farsi)

New Beginnings: Understanding the Basic Principles of the Christian Faith 2017 (Also available in Spanish, Farsi, and Japanese)

DEDICATION

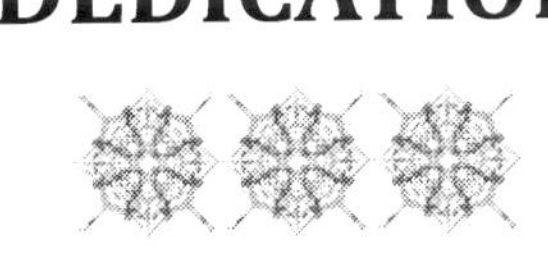

Simply Dedicated to everyone
who helped me step out of the miry clay
and set my feet upon
the Rock of Jesus Christ

CONTENTS

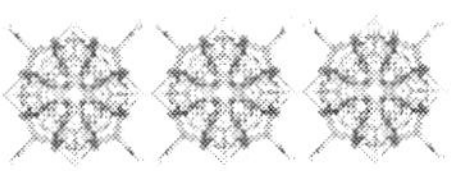

FOREWORD

About the Author

When I met Jesus on the floor of my prison cell many years ago, I could have never imagined He would - or could - restore my wretched life. From a past of addiction, homelessness, suicide attempts, prison, and self-hatred, God rebuilt my whole world into one of joy, peace, and purpose. Since I was miraculously saved, my "life verse" from the Bible has been Joel 2:25 ...."I will restore all the years that the locust have eaten". Locusts are pests that destroy everything in their way, and that was truly my life before Christ. There was nothing left to salvage.

I pray that you will believe He can do the same for you!

From My Pastor

For as long as I have known her, Sharon Dutra has demonstrated an unquenchable passion for Jesus. She has responded with a resounding Yes to the call of God upon her life. Sharon is pursuing a life of fruitful purpose and is now ministering to people in different parts of the world. Her success and the favor of God on her life is nothing short of supernatural. Her discipleship books have shipped throughout the United States, Africa, and Mexico. They have been translated into different languages so they can minister to audiences in places they would not usually have the ability to reach. Through it all, Sharon has maintained a humble, grateful, and loving heart. I am thankful to call her my friend and co-laborer in the Lord's Harvest.

Pastor Steve Henry
Harvest Church, Arroyo Grande, California

About This Book

First of all, I would like to say that this book would not have been written if God had not radically changed my life.

Secondly, I am certainly not worthy to write such a book. I have sin, problems, and issues in my life, as we all do. So I am not writing to point *at* you, but rather to take your hand and point you to our Lord. I am just grateful that He has given me the ability to explain spiritual truths so that people can more easily understand the deep concepts of the Bible.

Many themes have been repeated in this book. What I've written is what I have learned and been taught through Bible reading, prayer, and experience. It's what is ingrained in my heart and mind. This is the reason some themes are used so frequently.

Even the Bible says that we need to remember, and be reminded of scriptural truths regularly (John 14:26; 1 Corinthians 15:1). What may seem like trivial repetition is what actually solidifies thoughts and truths into our hearts and minds. Just as we study the same material over and over for a test, we are to repeatedly think about the things we have learned from the Bible.

The chapters have been purposefully chosen so that you can grow into strong believers and learn how to use your gifts to edify the church and reach out to the lost.

Fishers of Men was written in 2 parts. Part I is to help prepare your hearts to receive God's truth about your identity in Christ and the need to come under His leadership. It will ground you in your Christian beliefs. Part II was written to help train you to serve God and others in a meaningful and eternal way.

Fishers of Men is the sequel to my other books titled *Be Transformed: By the Spirit of the Living God* and *New Beginnings: Understanding the Basics of the Christian Faith.* Many people aren't taught how to "go to the next level" in their faith after they receive Jesus as their Savior. *New Beginnings* lays the groundwork. *Be Transformed* helps you apply spiritual principles to your life's issues. *Fishers of Men* is a more in-depth book about the spiritual and practical applications of the Christian faith.

I'll warn you now that you might not like some of the content of this book. It won't sit well with your sin nature. Many "Christ followers" like to justify their behavior by believing that God's grace will cover their fruitless Christian lives. But if you let the Holy Spirit speak to you through this book so you can grow and become more productive for God, you will reap many rewards.

The truth is, the American church has become far too complacent! We love to hear the part about God's love, blessings, power, and peace, but so often, we close our ears to the challenges of Christ to "take up our daily cross", and "die to our flesh".

I believe that the Church as a whole needs to be more grounded, more obedient, less complacent and less obsessed with "not being offensive".

Therefore, this next section describes my deep concern about the mediocrity and the lack of lost souls being brought into the Kingdom in this country. For this reason, *Fishers of Men* has been written.

Superficial Religion

There was a time in history when preachers boldly spoke the truth. The audience actually listened - even as they were being convicted or they felt uncomfortable. While it is true that some of these preachers could have used a bit more love and grace in their message, their sermons were powerful in converting the unsaved and motivating the Christian!

This type of convicting preaching is more often seen today in the persecuted church around the world, and in prisons and jails in America, than it is in the comfortable pews we often sit in every Sunday. In fact, thousands of my books are sent to prisons and jails in America, Africa, and Mexico, and we've had 3 stories of "mini-revivals" happening after they studied the books!

Ironically, the persecuted and the incarcerated groups are where we are seeing the most new growth in God's Kingdom! When the preacher isn't watering the Gospel down so the audience "won't be offended", true conversion and a believers' spiritual growth is much more likely to take place.

Please understand - I am not writing this to be judgmental. Rather, it is because I feel that we, as professed Christians, have been "playing church" far too long. We have adopted the world's "politically correct" philosophy, allowing the world to convince us that righteousness equates with "tolerance", and holiness is out-of-date. But this attitude has critically burdened and disabled Christ's intentions for His people and His Mission on this earth. Recent studies have shown that the "growth" in many American churches has been largely due to Christians moving from one church to another, with little increase from new converts (*https://www.baptiststandard.com/news/faith-culture/rapid-church-growth-through-conversions-uncommon*). March, 2019). We need to wake up and realize that we can no longer do "business as usual". There is an even greater wave of evil coming, and we can no longer "whisper" or ignore our warning to the unsaved or the backslider.

We are past the time when we can "hide our lamp under a basket" (Matthew 5:14-15). As Christians, we are the light of the world, just as Jesus was. People are much less likely to walk through our church doors as they were in the past. We need to go out and shout the Gospel from the housetops, as the Bible says (Matthew 10:27)! We must help people see the impending danger, and lovingly lead them into the safe harbor of Jesus Christ (Colossians 1:28).

I pray this book will allow you to move into a new dimension with Jesus. If you're living a self-centered, complacent Christian life, God wants to change you into a Christ-centered, on fire, ready-on-a-moment's-notice-for-the-Kingdom kind of follower! May we desire the Cross with the Crown, and learn to truly crucify our flesh, so we can become Dynamic Disciples of Jesus Christ - indeed, *Fishers of Men*, to this dying world!

Sharon Dutra
Grover Beach, CA
April 2020

How To Study This Book

We begin every Bible study in prayer, as it is the most important part of the study. We start by asking God to forgive us of our sins and to clear our minds of anything that may hinder His Spirit from teaching His truth to us. We ask Him to be our ultimate Teacher, and to lead, guide, and direct our class.

After prayer, we take turns reading a paragraph of the text out loud. Anyone can ask a question at any time, and I often stop throughout the lesson to highlight or explain the material. Anyone can refrain from reading if they choose.

We use the New Living Translation Bible, as (in my opinion) it is the most easily understood version that is still true to the original biblical text. We also look up every Scripture as it appears in the text. *Please* look up all of the Scriptures! I don't have the power to change your life, but God's Word does!

Additionally, don't feel like you need to rush through the book. We often spend a whole class on only one or two paragraphs! There is a lot of thought-provoking material in this book, so it's best if you just take a few sections per setting, and really spend time thinking and talking about them. If you just fly through it, you'll miss the deep truths that are written in them.

We often expound on the material by sharing our own insights, struggles, and victories. If you're not sure of a biblical truth, ask your pastor or trusted Bible teacher and bring it back to the group at your next meeting.

A Note To Those Who Are Reading This Book Individually

I have made the studies as easy to read and reference as possible, as I understand some of you won't (or don't want to) have a group setting in which to ask questions or share your knowledge. But as you work through the sections at your own pace, you'll learn a lot about yourself and your relationship with God.

Leaders or Facilitators

If you are the leader of the group, it's a good idea to familiarize yourself with the material before the class. You can either use the studies as a baseline for your own teaching, or you can act as a facilitator as the group works through the studies.

Just to clarify, I often use only one line out of a Scripture paragraph. This is intentional, and is not meant to take the idea out of the context in which it was written. Before I wrote that "one verse", I studied the surrounding context. But the verse fits well, and it perfectly drives home the point of which I am making. Of course, you and/or the group are free to read the text before and after the stated Scripture if you feel led.

At the end of each chapter, there are questions to ponder. There are no "right" or "wrong" answers, but they relate to something that was said in the text. They will help you explore your own beliefs, as well as solidify biblical truths in your heart and mind. Please take the time to write your answers down.

Contact Information

If you would like to purchase a book or write to me, you may contact me by mail at Post Office Box 597, Grover Beach, CA 93433.

Or email me at *betransformed@betransformedministries.com*

You can visit my website at betransformedministries.com

You can follow our ministry on facebook at facebook.com/ betransformedministries

If you'd like to see my radical life transformation story on YouTube, you can go to *https://www.youtube.com/watch?v=UuH8U_dRdiw*

If you find any spelling errors, I'd love to hear from you!

My books are available in English, Spanish, and Farsi (and soon to be in Japanese in the middle part of 2020). You can purchase the English and Spanish books on Amazon, or write me if you'd like one in Farsi or Japanese.

All books are free to those in prisons, jails, and rehabs. If you would like to donate to our ministry so we can send more books out, please contact us.

And if you truly cannot afford a book, just contact me and I will send you one. I have a special heart for those who are in a difficult place, as I was once in that position. May God bless you all richly.

PART I

THE HEART OF DISCIPLESHIP

CHAPTER 1

PASSION FOR JESUS CHRIST

PART 1

It is common knowledge that the church in America today
has become largely ineffective.
Why is this?
It's really a very simple answer.

**It is our lack of passion,
deep intimacy,
and sold-out commitment
for Jesus**

In this book, I would like to share with you the secret of being a true disciple – an authentic follower of Jesus Christ. Don't worry - it's not a "new revelation" I've had, and it's absolutely biblical.

Before we begin our study, there is a "Priority List" to fill out at the end of this chapter. Please go there now and thoughtfully consider your own priorities. This will help you to see where you truly stand in relationship to Jesus. Then we'll begin our study.

Becoming a Dynamic Disciple

As mentioned in the Foreword of this book, the process of becoming a Dynamic Disciple of Jesus Christ takes time, effort, discipline, and focus. The Christian life is simple, but it is *not easy*. Jesus offers us salvation freely, but the Bible makes it clear that without a change in our heart, attitude, behavior, and productivity for His Kingdom, our conversion may be suspect.

I would like to begin by exploring one of the most vital aspects of our Christian faith that we often overlook, and that is our **love** for Jesus. We tend to focus on what we *do* for God, but we can easily minimize the importance of just *being* in His presence. However, it is this very act of spending quiet time alone with the Lord that gives us vitality, strength, insight, and vision in our Christian walk.

In fact, it is much easier to *do* than to *be.* Both the secular and spiritual camps in our culture tend to be obsessed with activity, and we are practically shamed if we are not performing excellently in all aspects of our lives! Of course, there is a "tension" between relaxing in God's presence and working for His Kingdom, but it's important to find a healthy balance between the two.

His Precious Presence

As many people look back to the time when they first met their Savior, they often discovered that the intense love they experienced from Him and for Him was the very reason they began following Him. It's why many are willing to give up their lives for Him. If you had never received genuine, unconditional love and acceptance before, you may have found this new relationship to be one of the most thrilling in all of your lives.

Although as time passes, we may find that we continue to "follow" Him, but begin to feel like it's more of a chore than a joy to serve Him. We may start to focus on our "faith" or "outward behavior" or "gifts" more than on the *Person* of Jesus. Consequently, we may develop a type of "religious" shell, which, by Jesus' own accounts, He despises. This is because He desires deep intimacy with us, and this fake religious attitude distances us from Him. Additionally, this false behavior fails to draw the lost to Him, and instead, can easily turn them away from the Lord (Matthew 23:23-28). Indeed, our passion for Christ needs to be carefully guarded.

It is His love for us, and our return love for Him, that is really the foundation of our faith. Yet this is the part of the relationship that can be most easily damaged or ignored. Without careful attention, our affection for the Lord can wane, which hurts Him and robs us of the spiritual blessings He has for us. It also diminishes our service to others, because we become depleted of the love, joy, and peace we need as we minister to them in Jesus' name (Revelation 2:4-7; 3:15-16).

I pray that you are still in love with Jesus. But if you have lost your "first love" - if your love has grown cold - I hope this study will stimulate a new desire in you to put your flesh to death, and to put God back in His rightful place in your life. He is the only One who is entitled to your allegiance, and He is the only One who has the authority to be your King and Master!

Let's begin by examining how in love we are with Jesus. We'll start by describing how people act when they're in love

> *Usually, when people are in love, they act a little weird ☺ They have a hard time focusing on their daily routines, because thoughts of the other person invade their minds. They think up ridiculous ways to be with the other person. They don't care if they act a little strange - they have a deep longing to prove their feelings to their beloved. They stay up into the night talking, and then have energy to get their work done the next day. They don't mind spending their money on the other person. They plan their days according to what the other wants to do, and they never feel inconvenienced, even if they have to move their plans around, or do something they really don't care to do. They just want to be together.*
>
> ***Basically, their whole world revolves around the one they love***

So, in light of this description, ask yourself if this is how you feel about the Lord Jesus. If you realize your love for Him is diminishing - or that you have never even experienced this kind of crazy love for Jesus before - a change in your life may be needed if you really want to become a deeply loving disciple. This means being so committed to Christ that He becomes your first priority – your first love - no matter how difficult things get, or how awkward you may feel serving Him in your daily interactions. He doesn't want you to follow "religion". He wants a radical, fun, committed, overcoming, and fulfilling relationship with you!

God Wants ALL of Us

Many people with whom I have had the privilege of counseling and leading to Christ have said to me "Jesus was the very last Person I thought

I wanted in my life. I believed in 'God', but I absolutely avoided 'Jesus'". The amazing thing is that when I found Jesus, I realized He was the VERY one I was looking for"! This is because loving and knowing Jesus is the vehicle to a right and intimate relationship with the Father (John 14:6, 9). God is continually calling us into a deeper, more intimate, and life-changing relationship with Himself.

Since He first created Adam and Eve, He has made it clear from the beginning of time that He wants to be our NUMBER ONE priority. People who "claim" Jesus as Lord, but who don't really have a substantial relationship with Him, lack the vitality that marks a joyfully submitted Christian life. They know "of" Him; they speak as if they love Him; they go to church - they "look" like Christians....but....

How much of their time, talent, money, thought-life, and affection do they really give to God.... *compared* to how much they involve themselves in the world or spend on their own pursuits? How do they act, what language do they use, what is their attitude? How do they handle hardship? And how evident is the Holy Spirit's fruit in them - love, joy, peace, patience, kindness, goodness, faithfulness, gentleness, and self-control (Galatians 5:22-24)?

When Jesus says "Follow Me", He isn't saying "Just straggle along enough to keep yourself out of trouble". He is talking about a lifestyle that is fully engaged and deeply enveloped in Himself. He wants us to cultivate such a *profound relationship* with Him that we begin to have <u>His</u> mind and heart. He wants us to possess a joyful desire to do His will. He wants us to be *consumed* with Him!

Stop here and think about your relationship with Jesus. Be honest. Are you:

- Ignoring Him most of the time
- Letting Him "tag along" sometimes
- Intermittently allowing Him into your life, or
- Passionately loving and serving Him with most of your life?

<u>**Oh, That's Nice For *You*...**</u>

People occasionally tell me that my life-encompassing relationship with Jesus "is fine for you, but it's not for everyone". However, that's not what I read in the Bible! Right from the beginning, God tells His people that "He will have NO other gods before Him" (Deuteronomy 5:7). Our "gods" today can be our spouse, our kids (this is a common one), our job, our money, our appearance, the internet, sports, social media, cell phones, television, pets, addictions, other people's opinions...and we all know that the list goes on and on!

This same command to honor God above all else in the Old Testament also held to be true thousands of years later when Jesus arrived on earth. And it's absolutely relevant today. Jesus said "If you want to be my disciple, you must **hate** everyone else - by comparison - your father and mother, wife and children, brothers and sisters - yes, even your own life. Otherwise, you cannot be my disciple (Mark 8:34-38; Luke 14:26; 18:29-30; John 12:25-26).

The word "hate" in this verse in Luke is not the common meaning we usually think of when we hear the word, but rather, "loving Jesus SO MUCH MORE than anyone else that it almost *seems* like hatred in contrast. He makes it clear that we will not be counted as His disciples if we don't purposefully choose Him - FAR above everything else!

It's not a matter of having God conveniently fit into our relationships and plans, or allowing Him occasional Lordship. Jesus is saying "There should be NO contest - no competition - no rival for *My rightful place* in your heart, mind, spirit, or will". We shouldn't even place God and people in the same category. He belongs in His very own, exalted, solitary, and singular place in our lives. *Everything and everyone else* should pale by comparison.

And He isn't grandstanding! He knows that if we put Him and His Kingdom first, we will finally have the joy, peace, restoration, hope, purpose, and love we have been searching for. And IF we choose to follow Him first, He promises that He will handle the rest of the details in our lives that we tend to be so consumed with (Matthew 6:31-33).

It's a Lifestyle, Not a Vacation....

Returning to our passage in Deuteronomy 5, we find a very interesting statement that God made in verse 6. Right before He gives Moses the Ten Commandments, we are told why He has the authority to demand full allegiance from His people. It's because He *rescued them from slavery.* He is their Deliverer and their Savior! It's no different with us today. We have been bought with the precious price of Jesus' blood – rescued and delivered from *our* slavery to sin (1 Peter 1:18-19). He is entitled to our absolute devotion in return!

God also calls His people *wholeheartedly* to Himself when He says "You must not have any other idols" (Deuteronomy 5:8-9). Because of His magnificence and power, He has the right to demand that our primary affection be for Him.

The Lord goes on to warn us not to use His Name in vain (Deuteronomy 5:11). This can be taken even more seriously than just using His Name as a swear word - it's also flippantly throwing His Beloved Name around in our lives without properly representing Him and giving Him the adoration and deep respect that He deserves (Psalm 111:10; Proverbs 9:10).

God then commands us to keep the Sabbath Day holy (Deuteronomy 5:12). Why? Because He wants to spend time with us! He is a God of relationship. He desires that we purposefully set aside our daily work and concerns for one day of the week, because He intends for us to rest - *in Him.*

I'm sure we have all experienced weekend "family" time. But nowadays, everyone seems to be on the phone, computer or television, distracted from the *relationships* within the family. Intimacy and authentic connection is discarded for entertainment's sake. Sadly, that time is lost, not enriched. And this is how God feels when we ignore Him for lesser pursuits.

Additionally, God has made a way for us to *live* in that Sabbath (spiritual) rest seven days a week, as the Holy Spirit indwells us (Hebrews 4:1-11). The Lord knows full well that we will be the most alive, the most joyful, and the most productive **as** we live in this intensely intimate connection with Him on a daily basis (Deuteronomy 6:4-9).

We have great responsibility in our relationship with God. Our primary goal should be focused on getting closer to Jesus. Many people strive to "keep all the rules", but this always results in futility and shame. *True* faith flows from our heart and becomes the strength of our life. When we allow the Spirit to empower us, our ability to obey the Lord becomes much easier, because our vitality now comes from *His* mighty power, not our own (Haggai 2:4-5; Zechariah 4:6).

The supernatural love that God imparts to us when we draw close to Him will give us the confidence and power we desperately need in order to do as He asks of us. He won't leave us alone to figure life out by ourselves, and He doesn't leave us helpless.

We only become helpless when we put ourselves on the throne.

There are many people who may seem like they are powerful and successful without the Lord. But in reality - in the grand plan that God has for mankind - they are similar to the Wizard of Oz....a person hiding behind a facade of grandeur. In God's eyes, they are failing in the one thing that *really* matters in this life and in eternity - having a passionate relationship with His Son Jesus.

Again, the secret to Christian living is to "Love the Lord God (first), with all of your heart, all your soul, all your mind, and all your strength". (Mark 12:29-30). In our culture today - yes, even in the church - we spend far too much time loving ourselves first. In fact, a large percentage of the American Church is in love with Herself, and that is why she has become so ineffective at reaching the lost.

How Do I Know if I Am Living for Myself or for God?

Putting God above all else creates a foundation for our lives, a sturdy support upon which everything else is built. If He is not your number One priority, the bedrock of your life is faulty. And it will not provide the endurance you will need to live in godliness during the storms you encounter (Matthew 7:21-27). God wants your life to be stable and full of purpose for His Kingdom, and He knows that He's the only one who has the power you need to make that happen (Philippians 2:13).

Let's read Romans 8:5-14 below, which clearly reveals to us whether we are serving God or ourselves. I have included the Scripture here (italics mine):

"Those who are dominated by the sinful nature think about sinful things, but those who are controlled by the Holy Spirit think about things that please the Spirit. So *letting* your sinful nature control your mind leads to death. But *letting* the Spirit control your mind leads to life and peace. For the sinful nature is always hostile to God. It never did obey God's laws, and it never will. That's why those who are still under the control of their sinful nature can never please God. But you are not controlled by your sinful nature. You are controlled by the Spirit *if* you have the Spirit of God living in you. (And remember that those who do not have the Spirit of Christ living in them do not belong to him at all.) And Christ lives within you, so even though your body will die because of sin, the Spirit gives you life because you have been made right with God. The Spirit of God, who raised Jesus from the dead, lives in you. And just as God raised Christ Jesus from the dead, He will give life to your mortal bodies by this same Spirit living within you. Therefore, dear brothers and sisters, you have no obligation to do what your sinful nature urges you to do. For if you live by its dictates, you will die. But *if*, through the power of the Spirit, you put to death the deeds of your sinful nature, you will live. For all who are led by the Spirit of God are children of God".

This passage makes it clear that if we are living only for ourselves, we will experience:

spiritual death
rebellion towards the things of God
hostility in our relationships
lack of desire and ability to please God, and
an inability to overcome fleshly cravings, attitudes, and behaviors
(Galatians 5:19-21).

But if we are living in the Spirit, equipped with His power, we will continually think about ways to please God. We will be full of life – with an abundance of love, joy and peace. We will know with confidence that we are in good standing with the Lord, and we'll have a clear conscience (1 Timothy 1:5).

Our relationships will be more tranquil. We won't be so overcome by thoughts and behaviors that we know are displeasing to Jesus. Instead, we will glorify God by exhibiting the beautiful fruit of His Spirit. We will fall in love again with our Beautiful Savior. And it won't be a fight to do so.

CHAPTER 1
PASSION FOR JESUS CHRIST
PRIORITY LIST

Rate each of these categories in the order of importance to you on a scale from 1-5, 5 being the most important. It will help if you consider how much of your time, money, thought-life, and effort you put into each category. If a category does not apply to you, just leave it blank.

- MONEY 1 2 3 4 5
- CHILDREN/FAMILY 1 2 3 4 5
- SPOUSE (Or Boyfriend/Girlfriend) 1 2 3 4 5
- GOD 1 2 3 4 5
- YOURSELF 1 2 3 4 5
- SEXUALITY 1 2 3 4 5
- APPEARANCE 1 2 3 4 5
- HOBBIES 1 2 3 4 5
- SPORTS 1 2 3 4 5
- JOB 1 2 3 4 5
- ENTERTAINMENT 1 2 3 4 5
- CHURCH/RELIGION 1 2 3 4 5
- POPULARITY 1 2 3 4 5
- EDUCATION 1 2 3 4 5
- PETS 1 2 3 4 5

CHAPTER 2

PASSION FOR JESUS CHRIST

PART 2

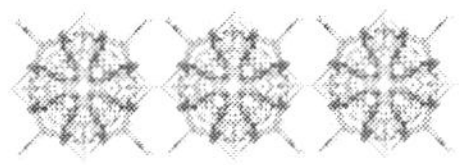

How Do I know if the Holy Spirit is Alive in Me?

The interesting thing about the Kingdom of God is that it is so opposite from our human ways. Indeed, the Bible says that the Gospel will sound like foolishness to the ungodly (1 Corinthians 1:18-31). God, in His wisdom, reveals to us a radically different way to live: "We must die in order to live". "We must give in order to receive". "We must sacrifice in order to have everything we really crave". "We must surrender in order to be free".

And this is where we often fall short. We don't want to suffer for anyone, or sacrifice anything we have. Many times, we fail to let Him have His way with us, because we allow our flesh, the world, and the devil to get the upper hand in our lives. We must admit that often, WE come first in our lives, not the Lord.

On the contrary, when the Holy Spirit **controls** our life, the expression of Christ in us is so evident! We become more patient and kind, loving and wise, generous and joyous.

Stop here and answer these questions:

- Do you really *know* the Holy Spirit?
- Are you afraid of Him?
- Do you think you will lose control of your life, or that you will look foolish if you give Him more dominion over your life?
- Is there evidence that He is at work in your life? How can you tell?

I will be the first to confess – it's not always easy being a Christian! The Bible tells us to CRUCIFY our flesh! To deny ourselves! This usually isn't fun. But when we stay in our two-year-old mentality of "Me" and "Mine", we are never satiated. We "pout and scream" to get our way, and throw a tantrum when we don't. The problem with this attitude is that we will always want more - we will never be satisfied. Additionally, everyone knows this kind of behavior is not pleasing to be around ☹.

God wants us to mature so that we think of others *at least as much* as we think of ourselves (Philippians 2:3). This includes benefitting people outside of our family *and* our church. However, overcoming our self-centered nature is only accomplished by God's work in us, as we commune with Him regularly.

A good indicator of the Spirit's power in us is how others relate and respond to us. Are people asking us why we are so happy, or peaceful? Are they open to us sharing Christ with them, because they see the love we have in our hearts for them? Do non-believers act more positively and respectfully around us than they do with their other friends? Are people attracted to the luscious fruit of God's Spirit in us?

Am I Really a Christian?

Referring back to Romans 8 (please read verses 9-14 again), we see in verse 12 that Paul is speaking to Christians here, as he addresses them as "dear brothers and sisters". But why would verse 9b say "IF" you have the Spirit of God living in you" - if they were already believers? He goes on to say "if you don't have the Spirit living in you, you don't belong to God at all"!

Furthermore, this passage says that we will live IF we live by the Spirit and put our flesh to death. This relationship with God is given to us as a free gift, but many of the benefits we are promised are conditional (check out all the "ifs" in this chapter!).

Therefore, we need to ask ourselves "Am I really right with God"? Am I *truly* living for Him – or is it just lip service? Am I accessing the Holy Spirit's power and regularly living like Jesus? This is not to make us feel condemned. But it should stop us in our tracks, as we consistently and honestly examine our lives to see IF the Spirit is really at home in us (2 Corinthians 13:5).

As 21st century Christians, we need to realize that human behavior hasn't changed much since the Fall in the Garden of Eden. The Bible - God's perfect handbook to mankind - is an expert in human behavior. As we study it, we find that we may have a grave "spiritual weak spot", one in which we are able to live a life that looks and sounds like we are followers of Christ, but it can be totally devoid of the Spirit. That's a sobering thought. The Scripture we read in Romans also says that we are made right with God WHEN (and only when) we have the Spirit in us. This is because He is the One Who gives us real life - the kind of life that is compatible with a relationship with our holy God.

While it is true that we receive eternal life and the Holy Spirit when we accept Jesus into our hearts, over time, we may become like those described in the Parable of the Soils (Matthew 13:18-23). We may have accepted Jesus, but a sustained, intimate relationship with Him, as well as fruit in our lives, is *proof of the reality* of our salvation decision (James 3:13; 2 Peter 1:10).

As we influence people for Jesus, and lead them into salvation and discipleship, we actually produce eternal fruit. We need to be mindful about the possibility of snuffing out the work of the Holy Spirit in our lives, thus making *us* not only ineffective, but possibly even turning people away from Christ (Ephesians 4:30; 1 Thessalonians 5:19).

We find Scriptures that speak of those who think they are going to heaven, but when they come face-to-face with Jesus, He says "Depart from Me, I never knew you" (Matthew 7:21-23; Luke 22:13-27). You might be thinking at this point that I am finding passages just to induce shame. But if you read the gospels, most of the stories have exactly the same theme - *"Repent and have a life-changing, radical relationship with Jesus"!*

As Christians, we are to manage our lives well so we will not bring Him shame on this earth, or bring ourselves shame on the day of reckoning (1 John 2:28). Our Lord wants us to fall head-over-heels in love with Him so we will glorify Him, bring others to Him, and have abundant life!

That Elusive "Abundant Life"

There are many reasons why we don't have the abundant life that Jesus speaks about in John 10:10. It certainly is not a life where we sit in our easy chairs and receive every blessing we (think) we want (Luke 12:14-21). This "abundance" isn't about us being overly blessed so we can enjoy life, as much as it is being so abundantly filled with love, peace, joy, and hope that it spills out of us to attract this dying world to Jesus.

This Scripture in John 10 is talking about a Spirit-filled life; in essence, "Real Life"! Our sin nature believes that everything *except* Christ will make us happy. This is a lie, one that I'm sure you have sadly experienced at some point in your life. In reality, how often have the people, places, and things you have pursued apart from God brought you true happiness and fulfillment?

Indeed, the Bible says that "Whoever has the Son has life; whoever does not have God's Son does not have life" (1 John 5:12)! This *life* is one of joy, vitality, excitement, generosity, overcoming power, and peace. Scripture makes it clear that we may be physically "alive", but unless Jesus has become our most important relationship, we are really "dead" on the inside (Ephesians 2:1-5; Colossians 2:13).

I have heard many people praying, asking God for to "bless" them - in essence, to "hand over" the abundant life. They are looking for feel-good experiences, but they don't want the "hard work" of crucifying their flesh, taking up their cross, and truly following and obeying Jesus. Instead, they pray for more money and less struggles. But their focus is completely on themselves! Of course we should pray for everything and without ceasing. But we also need to let God be God, and allow Him to answer our prayers according to HIS will.

The Abundant Life is realized when we begin asking God what *we* can do for *Him,* not the other way around. All too often, our problems and our desire for gratification become the sole focus of our relationship with Him. We begin to worship the "gifts" rather than the Giver of the gifts.

Flesh or Spirit?

We live in a society that exalts everything that is contrary to God. But God wants to create us "anew" in Christ Jesus, so we can do the things He planned for us long ago, even before we were ever born (Ephesians 2:10). "The things He planned for us" includes living a life where we glorify Him and influence others for His Kingdom. We do this by *choosing* to live out His purposes, by His Spirit's power – every single day.

Now I realize that some of you might be thinking "How in the world can I fit this all-encompassing relationship with Jesus into my life? I can barely maintain the life I have without adding one more thing to it". The answer lies in our priorities. If we are struggling only to keep up with our busy schedules and fulfill our own desires, we will likely find that we are running on our "flesh", not by the power of the Holy Spirit. This will cause assured burnout!

When our primary focus is on this world, we are placing our trust in things that are false. When we are empowered only by our own will, strength, and decisions, frustration is usually the norm. However, when God is our priority, we receive **His** power and **His** wisdom. Things run much more smoothly, because we now have Someone who is all powerful and knowledgeable to help us, direct us, and care for us.

- Are you building your own "kingdom" here on earth, or are you more concerned with building God's Kingdom? Which do you think is more important?

What Are Some Ways We Can Become More Dynamic Disciples of Jesus?

1. Get Rid of Our Idols (Colossians 3:5)

An idol is *anything that takes the majority of your time, talent, thoughts, affection and money away from God - the One Who deserves it the most.*

One way to change your thoughts and behavior is to begin by praying and asking God what it is He wants to change in you. Then focus on that one area of needed change and start eliminating it every day for a week or two.

Then add another thing the next week.

For example, let's say you want to quit smoking (or any other idol/ addiction). Start cutting down a few cigarettes a week for a month, until you stop. Of course, there is certainly nothing wrong with quitting an addiction or throwing an idol out at once, either! You can write in your own vice or ungodly habit in this section.

Attitudes are more difficult to destroy. We often have a hard time seeing ourselves as we really are. We like to think of ourselves as "nice people", but we all have displeasing facets to our personalities. Maybe it's pride, or selfishness, or lust, or rudeness, or coarse language that is your sinful bent.

One way to handle this is to ask a trusted friend (one who will be honest with you!) to point out your blind spots. You can look these attitudes up in the Bible and read the related Scriptures. Humbly ask God where He might want to highlight your sin and work with you to change.

The Bible says that there are three main ways we can become obsessed with the things of this life: "For all that is in the world, the lust of the flesh and the lust of the eyes and the boastful pride of life, is not from the Father, but is from the world" (1 John 2:16 NASB).

The *lust of the eyes* may be pornography or materialism -things you see that you want to obtain. The *lust of the flesh* may be immoral sexual practices or overindulgences. And *the pride of life* is basically saying you don't need God – that you are perfectly capable of running your own life. It's trying to receive the credit and glory for much of what God gave you the ability and talent to accomplish in the first place.

The principle here is to *lessen* the power our idols have over us. Maybe God has revealed a personality trait or habit in you that is contrary to what the Holy Spirit desires. Become aware of it by asking God and others in your life to lovingly make you accountable for your sins, habits and attitudes. Decide to act and react in the ways of the Lord - with love, joy, patience, kindness, gentleness and self-control. Little by little, you will notice a difference. It's not easy, and by all means, this takes great help from God!

2. Practice LOVING GOD

Getting rid of our idols will free us up to spend more time, energy, affection and resources on loving God and to develop more intimacy and affection for Him. Know that it will be difficult as you begin making these adjustments – this is a lifestyle change and it will take time.

We can actually pray for the desire to love God more! It is His will that you adore Him, so He will surely help you to do this! I like to close my eyes when I'm in my private prayer time and actually picture God the Father, God the Son, and God the Holy Spirit. Although the Father and the Spirit are Spirit and not body, I still think of them in terms of people I can see. This helps me to focus on their greatness, their royalty, and their beauty.

Pray throughout the day that God would reveal the things He wants you to do, and the people He wants you to share Jesus with.

This helps us to love Him more, because it makes us more mindful of the important things in life and helps us to realize that our lifestyle choices have eternal outcomes. Purposefully focusing on our God, and desiring to love Him and please Him also brings HIM great joy ☺

3. Read the Scriptures Daily

One of the best ways to get to know God and to fall in love with Him is to learn how to read your Bible. This is an *essential* part of being a disciple of Christ. One of my favorite books that helped me study the Bible when I first became a Christian is *What the Bible is All About* (Henrietta Mears 1983). I also wrote a chapter on "What is The Bible?" in my previous book called *New Beginnings: Understanding the Basic Principles of the Christian Faith* (Sharon Dutra, 2017; Amazon).

Reading and meditating on the Scriptures has the power to change our minds and our lives. The Bible is alive and powerful and is able to discern the thoughts and intentions of the heart (Hebrews 4:12). This means that it can uncover sin and align our thinking with God's thoughts and intentions!

4. Pray Continually

This means being aware of God and His involvement in our lives throughout the day. We can pray in our minds. We can also take a short walk or even a trip to the bathroom if we are at work or school, and we need to get with the Lord. We can pray for others as we come in contact with them all day long. Never underestimate the power of prayer. Don't forget - you're talking to GOD!

How Can We Learn To Love God More Effectively?

Consider these Scriptures from Jesus' teachings:

- Jesus says "My nourishment comes from doing the will of God" (John 4:34). We are literally "fed" in our spiritual lives by doing what He asks us to do! True Disciples of Jesus need to remember this verse, too. We often get so wrapped up in our daily lives that we forget the big picture-that God saved us to glorify Himself, and to bring others to Him. We are strengthened and enriched when we do His will. And we will never be more fulfilled than living the way He wants us to.
- Jesus speaks of "abiding" in Him and the subsequent fruit that we bear from this intimate relationship in John 15:1-8. The "fruit" from our authentic spiritual walk with the Lord is not only the spiritual enrichment we gain, but it is also the people we have influenced that will be with us in eternity (John 4:36).

  Just a note on our previous Scripture in John 15:7: Jesus says "But if you remain in Me and My words remain in you, *you may ask for anything you want, and it will be granted"* (italics mine). Some people take this particular verse out of the context of this passage and say "See? He'll give me whatever I want!" However, if you read the first part of the sentence, He says "**If** you *remain in Me and My Words remain in you..."* This speaks of an intimate relationship where we are following HIS will and HIS Word (the Bible). When we have His heart and mind, we will ask things according to His will, not our own.

  There is NO MORE IMPORTANT business that we should be about on this earth than affecting others for Christ, winning their souls for salvation, and discipling them in the faith. Also, living a life of holiness is a powerful witness to unbelievers and weak Christians alike. The Bible says that genuine disciples of Jesus will be living examples of His power - displaying confidence, a clear conscience, sincerity, grace, and wisdom (2 Corinthians 1:12; 1 Timothy 1:5; 3 John 1:11).

- Authentic life comes from "feeding" on Jesus (John 6:57). If we feel dry, weak, or ineffective in our Christian walk, our lack of intimacy with Jesus is likely the root problem. Not only is Bible study and prayer essential, but "feeding on Jesus" means consistently spending quality time with fruit-bearing, Spirit-filled Christians.

  It also includes being active in our Bible-based church, being baptized, tithing, and taking communion (again, there is more in-depth information on these subjects in my book *New Beginnings: Understanding the Basic Principles of the Christian Faith*). However, we do these things **only as** we are in relationship with God throughout each day. It's the "love relationship" that should motivate us to serve Him. As I've previously said, if we are missing this love link, it will become religion ☹
- Learning to love Jesus more passionately also means listening for His voice when He asks us to reach outside of ourselves in service to others. As we do this with Christians, we build up the Body of Christ. When we love and serve the unsaved people in our lives (our family, neighbors, grocery clerks, waitresses, bosses, co-workers, etc.), we earn the right to tell them about Jesus.

  If we are living in disobedience, we may not get the chance to tell them about our relationship with God, because they will see or sense that we are hypocrites. And to be sure, they have seen plenty of this kind of behavior.

Our Attitude is a Choice

How do we live in the Spirit? How can we become grateful instead of complaining? How will we become motivated to live for Christ every day?

- One way we can do this is by living in constant gratitude. Gratefulness goes a long way in helping us to love God. Begin thanking Him for every single thing in your life. We can do this by waking up in the morning and immediately saying "Thank you Lord for another day". We can get out of bed and realize that He has allowed our bodies to function today. We see the stars, the sun, the moon, the trees and flowers, our loved ones, etc., and say "Thank You, Lord, for all the beauty in my life".

When we go into the cupboard for food, we can say "Thank You Lord, for your bounty". Thank Him for your health, your marriage, your children, your car, your home, your job, the joy of your salvation and eternal life, freedom, your friends, your church, and anything else you think of or see during the day. If you actually thank Him for every gift you have in your life, you can develop a true heart of gratitude.

Even when I was incarcerated, I found plenty to thank Him for! I had Him by my side, I had the Bible to read, I had food and a place to sleep, I had a church to attend, and I was influencing others for His sake.

- Listen to Christian music. Train your mind to think upon lovely, true, and worthy things (Philippians 4:6-9). It's a habit that you'll need to cultivate if you want to experience victory and joy. Indeed, one of the many byproducts of joy is *strength* (Nehemiah 8:10)!
- Another way to become more like Jesus is to train our minds to reject negativity. Purposefully reject the enemy's attempts to rob your peace and joy. He will try to use the cares of this world to overwhelm you. We must also limit our exposure to negative people, even if they are our family, or our brothers and sisters in Christ. We truly do "become" who we spend the majority of our time with.

The lost people in this world do NOT want to be around complaining, dejected, sad, gossiping, or depressing people! The way to win souls to Christ is to have a smile on your face and praise on your tongue! THAT is attractive! Especially to the masses of people who have so many problems and who live in such fear and sorrow.

So, the bottom line is this: IF we want to have a life of full satisfaction, joy, and power, **it is our choice**. We cannot *make* ourselves happy, but we *can* choose to focus our minds on God's purposes and plans. And the best part is that we are not left without help. The Holy Spirit is ready and willing to fill us with exuberant life. He can help us achieve the purposes that God has planned for us since before He created the earth. But we have to *choose* to want more of Him and less of ourselves.

Follow Jesus! Imitate Him. Love Him with all of your heart. Seek Him in all that you do. And then you will become the *unique* Christ-follower - Christian - that He created you to be!

Perhaps today you can challenge yourself to begin spending more time with Jesus. You might need to get up earlier to do this. You can turn off the phone, the radio, the computer, or the television. It's ok to just sit there and think about Him! Talk to Him just as you would a close friend (that is actually called prayer!!) Why don't you determine to fall in love with Jesus? Seek Him, pursue Him, cling to Him. He WILL reward you with His Presence.

This is the stuff that ***real life*** *is made of* ☺

CHAPTERS 1 AND 2
PASSION FOR JESUS CHRIST
REFLECTION

1. **What is your estimation of your relationship with Jesus right now?**

2. **Do you believe that knowing Jesus more intimately and loving Him more deeply will improve your life?**

   Are you afraid of getting closer to Him?

   Are you afraid of giving Him more control of your life?

   Why?

3. **If you decide you want to move your priorities around, what are some changes that can help you put God in first place? (Take a class to help you learn how to share your faith; go to the gym less often; spend more time with genuine believers; join a small group Bible study; spend less time talking about your children/pets/money, job, etc; and talk/think more about God and His Kingdom)**

____

____

____

____

____

____

4. **If you want to truly put God first, you will need to make a concrete decision to do so. Time has a way of passing us by, and people, things, and events will crowd out our relationship with the Lord. You need to purposefully make time with Him every day. What are some practical ways you can do this? (i.e. Get up earlier, use the phone/computer/television less often, etc.)**

____

____

____

____

____

____

CHAPTER 3

TILLING THE SOIL

BREAKING UP THE FALLOW GROUND

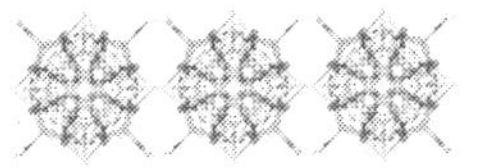

Have you ever considered that all the tools in your tool shed are dangerous? They can maim, disfigure, and even kill you! There's the rake, the shears, the hoe, and the hook. The lawnmower, the weed whacker, and the leaf blower can all cause harm if used improperly. Don't forget the spade, the shovel, and the hedge trimmer. Fertilizer can burn your skin. And insecticide can be fatal if ingested.

Yet, you may need all of these items in order to grow a beautiful, fruit and flower producing garden.

And then there's the 'work' aspect of gardening. As you dig and plant, your knees get stiff and your back aches. You sweat and generally get filthy. You are prone to cuts, scrapes, bites, stings, and punctures. Lastly, you need to continue doing all the work of weeding, pruning, watering, and fertilizing. And through it all, you aren't even sure that your garden will produce!

So, the question is: ARE ALL OF THESE RISKS AND EFFORTS WORTH IT?

God's Tools

We often avoid God's pruning work in our lives. But it's important to examine ourselves and decide to believe that when God is using His gardening tools to soften our hearts in preparation for us to receive good spiritual seed, water, and nourishment, that **IT IS** WORTH IT!

Let's consider some of the "tools" God uses to bring beauty out of our lives..... challenges, adversity, pain, friction and loss. He doesn't necessarily cause these things to happen, but He will certainly use them for our benefit (Romans 8:28). While these experiences are no fun, we see from our gardening story that this is often the very means that God uses to bring about the beauty of the finished product - which is godly character, and the fruit that we bear.

Tilling the Soil is all about breaking up the hardness of the ground and preparing it to receive seed, water, and nourishment. The Spiritual analogy is obvious. We must allow God to till the soil of our hearts regularly. The Old Testament speaks of "breaking up the fallow ground". The *fallow* ground was land that was left dormant for a year so that it could rejuvenate, which increased its potential for a greater harvest. However, during this dormancy, it was prone to gather thorns, thistles, and weeds. *The farmer needed to come in before planting and remove all of the potential hazards to the new crop.*

Jeremiah 4:3 says *"For thus says the Lord to the men of Judah and to Jerusalem, "Break up your* ***fallow*** *ground, and do not sow among thorns"* (NASB). The thorns choked out the good seed, and it was imperative that they be removed so the good seed could take root and flourish.

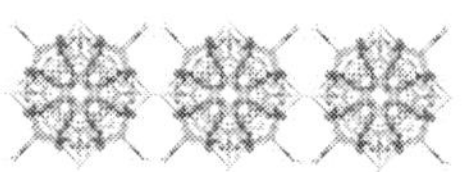

We probably all know this story of The Parable of the Sower, but it's so relevant to our spiritual lives today. Let's read Matthew 13:1-9 and18-23.

We see that the GROUND is the highlight of the story. That's because it's the only variable - the only thing that changes. All of the other conditions are the same - the Sower, the Seed, and the potential for the seed to be stolen, burned, or destroyed by the ways of the world.

Matthew 13:13-15 tells us that the *human heart* is like the GROUND. Our hearts can be in variety of conditions. They can be parched. They can be hard, not allowing any goodness to enter. And God's Truth can be snatched away from us. That is why Proverbs 4:23 tells us to "***Guard our hearts*** *above all else, for it determines the course of our* ***life***".

Of course, our hearts can be soft, as well. We can also have "soft" and "hard" areas in our hearts at the same time. What Jesus is talking about in this Scripture is *actively choosing* to let Him cultivate fertile soil in our hearts so that HE can harvest a fantastic crop - one that will bring **us** fulfillment and bring **Him** glory. We must identify the thorns in our lives if we want a harvest that pleases God.

So, the ultimate questions are: Will we truly submit our lives to Jesus, allowing Him to use any means necessary to make us more like Himself? And how much fruit will we produce? The answer to these questions are in direct proportion to the health of our hearts and our sustained surrender and obedience to Christ.

So, what is the Seed, the Water and the Nourishment in our lives?

We have already read that the essential ingredients for a bountiful, healthy crop are good seed, water, fertile soil, and nourishment. Let's see what the Bible has to say about these elements.

The Seed

Genesis 1:11 says "Then God said, "*Let the land sprout with vegetation - every sort of seed-bearing plant, and trees that grow seed-bearing fruit. These seeds will then produce the kinds of plants and trees from which they came.*"

Did you catch that? Even from the beginning, God created seed-producing fruit! As living creatures, human beings have the same potential. For example, we bear children - and they usually look and act just like their parents. The purpose of the seed is to bear fruit - and it is certain that we will bear fruit "according to that from which we came".

In other words, what we harvest is what we plant. If we sow into the flesh, we'll reap envy, division, idolatry, pride, and misery. And if we sow into the Spirit, we will reproduce love, joy, peace, and goodness.

Likewise, in a spiritual sense, God plants seed in our lives, and He expects it to grow and reflect HIS own character!

The Great Harvest

God uses the Bible, our circumstances, other people, and His Spirit to help us reproduce a luscious harvest that will help sustain us and others in our lives. Back in the story of the Sower, we find that the "seed" is the Word of God, implanted by the Spirit. As we read the Bible regularly, God is literally *planting potential crop* in our souls, minds, and hearts.

One sure way to develop deep roots is to study your Bible. Not just read it, but pray to receive God's message to you for that day. You can look up other Scriptures that have the same meaning as what you're reading. Use the concordance and dictionary in the back of your Bible to find similar themes. Searching the maps to find out where your text is taking place helps the Bible and its geographical location become more alive.

Ask God how your passage relates to your life and how He might want to change you. Really digging into the Word makes it stimulating and exciting! We need to realize that without this discipline, we will surely become dry, thorny, and rigid soil that will fail to produce life and fruit. Reading the Bible regularly, obeying it, and truly allowing it to change our lives gives us the power to live like Jesus (2 Timothy 3:16-17).

The Living Water

Did you know that a human being can survive without food for up to 3 weeks, but can only live without water for a maximum of 3 days? Nearly 60% of the body is made of water and every single cell vitally needs it. We all know that water keeps us cleansed and refreshed. Could that be one of the reasons why God Himself is referred to as the Living Water in the Old Testament, just as Jesus is in the New Testament?

Jeremiah 17:13 says *"O Lord, the hope of Israel, All who forsake You will be put to shame. Those who turn away on earth will be written down, because they have forsaken the fountain of* ***living water****, even the Lord".* And in John 7:38-39a, Jesus refers to Himself and the Holy Spirit by saying *"He who believes in Me, as the Scripture said, 'From his innermost being will flow rivers of* ***living water****'".* (*When He said "****living water****," He was speaking of the Spirit, who would be given to everyone believing in Him).*

How do we feel when we don't have enough water? Tired, thirsty, weak, and distressed. We can examine our spiritual health by asking ourselves if we have the Living Water flowing in us and through us. Are our lives an oasis where others can come and draw on Jesus, the Living Water? The Father wants Jesus and His Spirit to be gushing out of us – enough to refresh, restore, and rejuvenate others!

One of my favorite Scriptures is Psalm 1:1-3. It tells us that we will produce fruit *in all seasons* - but it is only "as we delight in the law of the Lord and meditate on it day and night". Also, being "planted by the riverbank" implies deep roots that are ready to handle floods, but at the same time, they are constantly enriched by running water. This is a picture of being *consumed* with God's presence, His ways, His plans, and His Spirit. When we are in intimate and regular communion with the Lord, He is magnified, because we shine with His great power, love, and glory. Great fruit can come from all seasons of a believers' life.

- How does this Scripture in Psalm 1 compare to my life? Am I overflowing with Christ's love and power, or am I drying up and becoming less interested in His Kingdom?

The Rich Nourishment

In John 4:34-38, Jesus explains where His vitality comes from. It says "Then Jesus explained: 'My **nourishment** comes from doing the will of God, who sent me, and from finishing His work. You know the saying, 'Four months between planting and harvest. But I say, wake up and look around. The fields are already ripe for harvest. The harvesters are paid good wages, and *the fruit they harvest is people brought to eternal life.* What joy awaits both the planter and the harvester alike'"! (italics mine)

The word "nourishment" here means literal food. It is the condition of being provided with the necessities of life. As we are active in DOING the will of God, it gives life to our bodies, minds, hearts, wills, relationships, and spirits. It sustains us, and gives us the ability to become strong and bold Christians.

Additional Essential Conditions for Fertile Soil

1. Living in humility, depending on God for absolutely everything
2. Staying in an intimate relationship with Him throughout every day and making Him the very highest priority in our lives
3. Communing with other strong, passionate believers

Humility

Humility is a vital ingredient to the "soil" that God is tilling in our hearts. The Bible says in 1 Peter 5:6 that "if we humble ourselves, HE will exalt us in due time". And James 4:10 says: "Humble yourselves before the Lord, and He will lift you up in honor".

I would rather humble myself than have my circumstances humble me! The loftiest position in the Kingdom is being a servant. And that's not just a nice saying from the Bible - it's really true (Matthew 23:11-12). I always say "If I'm humble, I'm closer to the ground and won't fall as hard".☺

I find it important to frequently ask myself: Does My Life Reflect Humility?

Here is an excerpt from the chapter on "Humility" taken from my book *Be Transformed: By the Spirit of the Living God:*

> *Humility is a picture of someone who draws their strength, peace, and direction from the Lord. It's one who knows their strengths and limitations, and still let's God be the Boss of their lives. It's someone who is so confident and secure in their position in Christ that they don't need to seek status, or exert their self-imposed power in every situation.*
>
> *The biblical definition of humility is far different than the self-centered qualities that our society embraces. Far from being weak, humility really means 'strength under control'. The English dictionary describes humility as being 'modest' or 'respectful'. It's really a lifestyle attitude of putting others before ourselves. And it requires great fortitude and self-control, because people who are humble before God consistently act in ways that are contrary to their sinful nature.*
>
> *They choose to love when they are hated. They decide to share their time, talent, and money, instead of hoarding everything for themselves. And they have God's power and courage to do good to others, even when they are faced with evil. It's no wonder that we have trouble finding those who display genuine humility.*

Also, as we humble ourselves, God is exalted. There can only be one person on the throne, and if we're trying to take that seat, the only thing others can see in our lives is "us". But when HE is enthroned, HE is the

One whose power and love shines out from us. I want *me* to be lesser so that He can be Greater! I already know what my life was like before God took control of it, and it's never pretty when I try climbing back on that throne!!☹

The second way we can keep our soil fertile is to stay in contact with Jesus throughout every day and make Him the highest priority in our life. "Busy-ness" can be one of the greatest enemies to our life in Christ. We are constantly bombarded with things we need to accomplish, places we need to go, and people we need to see. We work; we have spouses and children; we feel the need to be attractive at all times; we take care of household duties, pay bills, and a myriad of other things. Oftentimes, Jesus is the last Person we communicate with in our hectic schedules. And we wonder why we feel stressed, powerless, and guilt-ridden.

A great analogy of this concept was explained once when my Pastor gave a message about the wells in the Old Testament. One of the ways that Israel's enemies overpowered them was to fill up their water wells with dirt. Obviously, without water, the people died. This concept is so relevant to our lives today! We fill our lives with things that have no eternal value - and those things crowd out the life that Jesus is trying to impart to us - His Living Water.

Hosea 10:12 says *"Sow with a view to righteousness, Reap in accordance with kindness; Break up your* ***fallow*** *ground, For it is time to seek the Lord until He comes to rain righteousness on you"*. Hard ground cannot receive water! His righteousness will reign in us in direct proportion to the softness of our hearts. While God does the restorative and redemptive work in our hearts so we can receive Him, it is our job to keep ourselves pure (from the world) (2 Timothy 2:21).

A third way to keep our soil fertile is to spend quality time with other Christians who actually act like Jesus. Beware of relationships - even other "Christians" - that are toxic, negative, gossipy, or draining. Find believers who are nurturing, as well as those who are willing to keep you accountable.

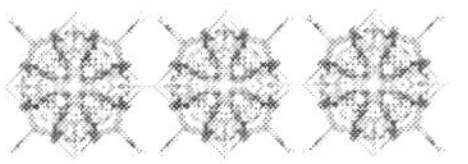

So, we have talked about allowing God to "till our soil" - welcoming His pruning techniques. Let Him have His way with you! Through our difficulties and daily irritations, relax and be mindful of your response to your stressors. We must surrender to God's leading - not forcing ourselves to be in control. Asking God's opinion about our decisions will bring clarity and positive direction. Making Him our first priority will literally simplify and enrich your life.

There are many circumstances we cannot change, but WE can change! It's so important to be prayerful and read the Bible. Throughout the day, thank Him....ask Him for His wisdom and His leading on your activities. Learn to turn off your computer or radio, or put down your phone and just *spend some time with Jesus!*

This message is not meant to add stress to your already-busy schedule! This is a PRIORITY that must happen! When we put HIM first, other things will work out in a much better way (Matthew 6:33). We will change, and we will start making eternal differences in the people around us. Jesus deserves our front-and-center devotion, and He knows we will function the best with Him at the forefront of our lives.

Maybe it would be helpful to write down what your average day looks like, and think about the activities that seem important to you, but they have no real value. Begin to be Kingdom minded and focused in your life. We need God's nourishment - which is doing His will - as we are His Ambassadors of salt and light to this world. These are the activities that are essential to your Christian life. Besides, they will bring you rewards that are far beyond your imagination!

CHAPTER 3
TILLING THE SOIL
REFLECTION

1. **Are you allowing God to use an adversity in your life to mold and shape you? Or do you frequently let yourself become irritated or disheartened by your circumstances?**

   ____

   ____

   ____

2. **Do you think that the trials you are now facing are a result of your poor choices, or of God's Divine training and pruning?**

   ____

   ____

   ____

3. **Am I doing the will of the Father? Or is my time mostly consumed with my own endeavors? The way to generally determine this is to write down:**
   1. What you spend your time doing:

   ____

   2. What you spend your time thinking about:

   ____

   3. What you spend your money on:

   ____

4. **What is the well-filling dirt in your life? These are the "fillers" that crowd out your REAL LIFE in Christ.**
   What are you so caught up with that it's crowding out your relationship with Jesus? (Most of these things are not negative by themselves, but if you spend so much time doing them that you're neglecting personal time with the Lord, you may want to take a look...)

Possibilities may include: Husband/Boyfriend? Children? Work? Ministry? Volunteering? Busy-ness? Religion? Computer/Phone? Pets? Your appearance?
Fill in your own answers here:

____

____

____

5. **What kind of fruit are you producing in your life right now that relates to bringing others to Jesus?**
   This can include the Fruit of the Spirit (love, joy, peace, patience, kindness, goodness, faithfulness, gentleness, and self-control); godly character; and drawing others to Christ by verbally sharing your faith with them.
   This can also include:
   Possibly changing the way you dress, the way you talk, the subjects you talk about with others; the way you treat others

   ____

   ____

6. **What kind of fruit would you *like* to be producing?**

   ____

7. **Determine 2 ways that you can begin bringing in a great harvest of lost souls for your Lord:**

   ____

   ____

8. **Name one thing you are willing to change in your life today to make God more of a priority.**

   ____

CHAPTER 4

LAYING THE FOUNDATION

PART I

Common sense tells us that we need a solid foundation for most situations in our lives. For instance, if we are to become a math major, we need the basic building blocks of excellent addition, subtraction, multiplication, and division. If we want to build a house, we need a strong base if we expect the house to last and not topple over. This concept is no different when we begin our life in Christ.

But this is exactly where many believers falter. They have no foundation in their Christian walk. They gladly accept Jesus at salvation, but oftentimes, they are not discipled and taught essential Christian truths. Therefore, they end up neglecting to learn Christian principles for themselves.

Thinking this job is up to the Pastor, they excitedly go to church and listen to the sermon every week. However, if believers are not trained to cultivate daily, private, and quality time with God and His Word, it is akin to eating only one meal a week!

Essential Training

Without this regular and intimate time with God, we can easily become confused and weak in our faith. If we hear and study God's truth only once or twice a week, we will have no choice but to believe all that the world is throwing at us. It is *vital* to make this meaningful, daily communion with our Lord a priority. Otherwise, we are apt to focus more on the "realities" of *this* world and on our day-to-day existence, than on God's plans and purposes for our lives. Most assuredly, if we are hearing the voice of the devil and the world for the majority of our waking hours, we will never be able to overcome our trials.

Furthermore, if our main input is negative and untruthful, we will become increasingly insensitive to the fact that there is a battle raging for human souls on this earth between God and Satan. Yet this warfare is of the utmost importance. We need to be armed and ready every single day - not only for ourselves, but for others who need Jesus. We desperately need God's Truth to counteract the mental, emotional, physical, and spiritual onslaught we deal with. Again, this is why we *must* become students of the Bible and prayer if we are to live the way that Jesus desires.

Because eternal lives are at stake, we as Christians should steadfastly focus on Christ our Rock, and then strive to make other people our *primary* concern in this life (Isaiah 26:3-4; Matthew 6:31-33; 28:18-20). As I often say, when we see our Lord face-to-face, the only part of our daily lives He will be concerned about is how we have used them to glorify the Father and bring others to Him.

Cruising or Battling?

There is no doubt about it - we are in a gruesome war. Even a casual observer can see that our world is becoming more frightening every day. But often, we Christians act like we are on a cruise liner instead of a battle ship! We like to think that since we are "saved", we are out of the woods – safe from Satan's attacks and headed for heaven. Really, though. Does a soldier enlist, train for months to go to war, and then take it easy when the bullets are flying?

It's the same principal with spiritual warfare. Salvation is only the first step of our Christian experience. It's the "signing up" part. We need to be aware that when we accept Jesus Christ into our lives, we are literally signing up for war! And there is no way we can fight in this battle without the necessary weapons (Ephesians 6:10-18). We are foolish if we fail to prepare for it, because a wounded, lazy, or uninformed soldier is of no help to his leader or his comrades.

Our main weapon is the Bible. Its timeless Truth is solid enough to build our life's foundation upon. But it won't do us any good if we only carry it into church each week (2 Timothy 3:14-17; Hebrews 4:12). We need to study it, understand it, and obey it as thoroughly as a soldier knows and follows his handbook and his orders - because it truly IS the difference between life and death.

Our second essential weapon is prayer. However, words uttered from the lips of one whose heart is unmoved for our Beautiful Savior, or is unimpassioned for hell-bound souls, will not move the heart of our God. Additionally, we often pray only for ourselves, and for our own will, but neglect to pray for others in our midst. Oh, that we may trade our hearts of stone for hearts of clay (Ezekiel 36:26-27). May we long for the things that God considers important.

This chapter, *Laying the Foundation,* will outline the essential biblical truths that need to be believed and put into practice before we can build on our Christian faith any further. It will speak heavily about *who we are in Christ*. Even if you've been a believer for many years, you may want to review these principles and shore up your own foundation of faith.

This teaching is imperative for the dynamic disciple of Jesus to grasp, because deeply understanding and believing what *GOD says* about who we are forms our "worldview". This worldview is basically our attitude towards everything that relates to our life and how we process it. Therefore, it significantly impacts how we love God and serve others in His name.

Our Position in Christ

People often wonder why Jesus is considered "The Only Way". They say "All religions lead to God". Or "It's so narrow-minded to believe that there is only one path". But God Himself tells us in His own words - the Bible - that in order to have intimate fellowship with Him, we have to *become* righteous. We are unable to avoid the darkness in our lives, or to live without sin (1 John 1:6-8).

Yet we need GOD to make us right with Himself, because we simply cannot make ourselves good enough to commune with a Holy God. If you think about it, this makes sense, because it's clear that as humans, we are fragile and fallible. We need Someone who is much greater than we are to save us and intercede on our behalf.

Our "position" in Christ can be seen in the analogy of someone designing or decorating a house. Each item is placed in a particular area with a purpose or a design in mind. Such it is with our specific arrangement in our Father's plan. He *places* us where He wants us, with our great purpose and His grand design in mind. It's not an arbitrary or last-minute choice– it is intentional. In fact, God wrote the "blueprint" for our lives before we were even born (Ephesians 1:3-8)! It is when we try to remove ourselves from His positioning that we feel out of place.

One of the most important realities that Christians must embrace is the fact that we have been loved, forgiven, equipped, and chosen by God since before time began. And while it is true that He loves every single human being just the same (John 3:16), He has a special place in His heart for those who genuinely love Him in return. It's amazing that He foreknew His followers even before the earth was made (Romans 8:29-30).

As we accept *God's* plans and purposes for our lives, it will help us to move past our preoccupation with ourselves. When we believe the fact that we are already beloved and belong to God through salvation, it will free us from having to search for approval. When we *truly internalize* that we are *already complete* in Christ, we can combat the myth that we need to be "good enough" for God. This is HIS truth - HE has *already declared* us good enough! This liberates us to serve Him with our whole being, because we don't have to wonder if we are sturdy or worthy enough for His calling. We can then get on with the work He has planned for us (Ephesians 2:9-10).

As we become healthy and secure in Christ, our focus will naturally turn outward to the suffering people we see around us. If we are His authentic followers, we will want to do whatever we can to influence those who need Him. As the Lord dwells in us and with us, we will begin to learn to love the things that *He* loves. We will then begin to understand why Jesus' primary mission was, and is, to seek and save the lost (Luke 19:10).

We all have a special, unique work to do for the Lord. He has already hardwired us for what He wants us to do for Him! In fact, we were *created* to live out **His** specific plan for us - and that's why we are never completely satisfied in life until we are in relationship with Him and fulfilling *His* will for our lives (Jeremiah 29:11). "Doing our own thing" takes us off course. The truth is, we will never experience fulfillment or reach our true destiny using our own game plan (Proverbs 14:12).

Armed with this knowledge, we become stabilized in our thinking, because we can be assured that He already has the Grand Design written, both for world events and for our individual lives. We can stop worrying and fretting about "how things are going to turn out". We will learn to seek His leading through His Word, His Spirit, and prayer. As we gain confidence, we can then boldly go out and invite others into the magnificent life that Jesus offers.

Who Am I?

At the moment we receive salvation (Romans 10:9), God, through His gracious Holy Spirit, *places us* into a position of right relationship with Himself (Genesis 15:6; Romans 5:21; 8:33). We ARE new creatures at conversion - because God has made us so, not because of what we have done, what we think, or how we may feel.

But this "belief" is more than a nodded consent or lip service – it's a brand new lifestyle empowered by God Himself (Ephesians 4:20-24). What a relief it is to know that it isn't up to us to climb the Kingdom ladder to perfection!

We are so often used to measuring our lives according to our feelings that when we don't "feel" like we are loved, holy, forgiven, or precious, we take that as truth. But our job is to **believe** what GOD says about us in His Word (2 Thessalonians 2:13-14). While it's true that our old natures will always be a part of us, and we will fall and fail at times, as believers, Christ's perfect work on the Cross has delivered us from the punishment that we deserve for our sin, once and for all (Hebrews 9:12; 1 Peter 1:2)!

The Gospel message makes it clear that when we are in love with Jesus, we will want to immerse ourselves in His presence and obey what He has instructed us in the Bible. God's Spirit Himself works in us the profound changes in our hearts and minds that we so desperately need. HE gives us the *desire* and the *power* to become pure, thus making us more like Jesus (Philippians 2:13).

As we **press into** this relationship with Him, *He* will work out the transformation that must happen so we can live in victory. Just know that it will take effort and work to maintain our relationship with God; it's a partnership, not a one-sided effort. God will do for us what we cannot do, but He will not do for us what we are able to do (2 Timothy 2:15; 2 Peter 1:10; Revelation 14:13).

Lastly, we must understand and embrace the truth that we will never "find ourselves" - as many self-help groups and books claim - without being in an intimate relationship with Jesus Christ. This is because we were created in the image of God. He alone knows the depths of our hearts and minds, and knows how we best function.

Human effort and psychology will never be able to plumb the deep places inside of us, our true motives and secrets. Only God can heal us fully and set us back on the path that has been determined for our lives since eternity past (Ephesians 1:4). He alone can give us the wisdom, strength, knowledge, and supernatural power to live in harmony with Himself, thereby bringing us peace, love, joy, hope, and purpose.

So let's delve into our subject and read about who God deems we are in Christ:

1. We are made Righteous...Romans 4:1-8. God loves people intensely. From the beginning of time, He has wanted fellowship with us. But as we all know, Adam and Eve rejected this relationship and instead, chose sin. This really translates into "having their own way" ☹ instead of living the way that God had intended.

By choosing their own methods, they could no longer associate with God intimately because of His absolute purity and holiness. In fact, because of this rebellion, the entire human race was ruined from then on. Every single person is now born into sin (Romans 3:9-19).

Furthermore, God says there is **no redemption** from our fallen state, except through Jesus Christ (Romans 3:21-26). There is no human payment great enough to erase our sin, and no human has the power to get another into heaven. This is precisely why Jesus, as God, died for us (Romans 4:20-25).

JESUS took the punishment we deserved - because get this - *only GOD could have handled His own anger at sin* - since that kind of anger (wrath) would have destroyed us. Therefore, God says that we who are saved are now righteous, which means that we are "fully right" in His sight. Because of His gracious Sacrifice, Christians are now holy in His eyes.

When He looks at believers, He sees the Blood of Jesus - the sacrificial payment - covering us. Christ literally died in our place. He bore the full weight of our sin, because of His great love for us. Instead of the punishment we deserved, He gave us freedom and a fully restored relationship with God the Father. Remember, it is **God** who makes us holy and blameless *for Himself*. Salvation is not earned, nor do we have to work for it (Romans 5:16; Colossians 1:22).

The Great Atonement

Please bear with me while I explain some Old Testament concepts. You may already know your Bible history, but I want to make sure all of the readers are familiar with the content. Some of the information may seem tedious, but maybe it can help you to formulate what you may need to say when you share your faith.

In the Old Testament, animal sacrifice was instituted by God as a way to make amends for human sin, and to show His people just how severe their sin really was. By seeing animal blood shed for their sin, they saw that sin exacted a heavy price - **a life**. The Bible says that "without the shedding of blood, there is no forgiveness for sins" (Leviticus 17:11; Hebrews 9:22). This system was never intended to *erase* sin; it simply "covered it" so God could associate with an unholy people.

It is important to realize that this sacrificial system was never intended to be permanent. It was a "word picture", if you will, of the Great Sacrifice that Jesus would make for the world centuries later.

Again, in contrast with these temporary sacrifices, Jesus made the final, once-and-for-all-time payment for sinners. Jesus, the Perfect Sacrifice, is God Himself. In fact, His name is Emmanuel, which means "God with us". He has literally *erased* the sins of those who have accepted Him, making them worthy to come into an intimate relationship with God (Romans 1:15-17; 1 Thessalonians 5:23). Through His Holy Spirit, who is also God, He now dwells within the believer. As a cleansed and holy people, Christians are now called "The Temple of the Holy Spirit" (1 Corinthians 6:19-20).

If we look back to the time when Jesus arrived in history, the Jews, who were God's chosen people, had already known for centuries about the necessity of a sin-sacrifice. So they understood the significance of Christ's death when He was crucified on the Cross. These old rituals in the Old Testament were meant to point to Jesus – who became the ultimate, perfect, and final sacrifice for the world. Yet many of them refused to believe in Him (Matthew 13:54-58).

So the righteousness given to those who accept Christ is accomplished completely through Jesus' blood sacrifice. The Bible says that during the Crucifixion, our Precious Savior was literally WEIGHED DOWN WITH THE WORLD'S SIN for 3 hours, as God poured out His anger for *human sin* on Christ, the Sinless One (2 Corinthians 5:21).

That's why Jesus said "My God, My God, why have you forsaken Me?" when He was hanging on the Cross. He and the Father had had an endless, deep, and intimate communion throughout the ages, but at that moment, God could not associate with His Son while He was the Sin-Bearer (Matthew 27:45-46). Now we are able see this beautiful picture of what Jesus did for us.

Jesus Christ extends forgiveness for our sins, which is the path to a restored relationship with God and others. As we bask in His forgiveness, our guilt is erased, and we feel free to be close to Him.

Consider that God is deeply grieved when we refuse to receive the gift He offers of salvation and eternal life. Rejecting this kind of love is like a story of you dying as you're saving someone's life...but the person you rescued is completely ungrateful and tells everyone they saved themselves!

Finally, only JESUS was able to become the Great Sacrifice, because our mere sacrifices (even our very lives) were not flawless enough to be a satisfactory sacrifice to God. He required a Perfect Life, one without spot or wrinkle (Leviticus 22:17-20; Romans 8:1-4; Hebrews 9:13-14). Jesus, *as God*, was the only One who could fill that requirement. That's why Jesus tells us that He is the ONLY way to the Father (John 8:24; 14:6).

What is so interesting is that there were over 300 prophecies about Jesus thousands of years before He was even born! In the Old Testament, He is called "The Messiah", which means "Anointed". So the Jewish people had no excuse for not recognizing and accepting Him. However, they were so entrenched in their pride, power, selfishness, and money that they rejected the very One who came to save them.

And this is still true in our world today (1Corinthians 1:18-25). It has been said "You MUST do *something* with Jesus - that is the most important decision you will ever make". The truth is, either people are offended by Jesus; or they think that believing in Him is foolishness; or they accept Him as Lord and Savior.

As we read these Scriptures, we can understand the reason why Jesus was so upset with the Jewish religious leaders of His day. He was trying to show them that their man-made rules and regulations were worthless in bringing people to genuine repentance and fullness of life. It was through faith in *Him* that that they would find intimacy with the Father (Galatians 2:16). Faith is what would make them right with God - not their rituals and religion (Romans 5:1-2)! People still struggle with this concept today.

While spiritual "head" knowledge is important- we must study and understand the Scriptures – it is only as we allow this knowledge to sink into our hearts and control our minds and wills that it will become useful. Humans are notorious for trying to substitute cerebral information for a deeply personal connection with Jesus. But He will not be fooled. He wants our entire being (Mark 12:29-30).

Why is Our Faith So Important?

Being "made righteous by God" is a legal principle called "imputing". It is our English word for "assign" or "accredit". Think of it in terms of a royal heir. The son is *born into* his title. Even if he doesn't *act* like a prince at times, he IS a prince!

It's amazing that when we genuinely accept Christ into our hearts, we are *born into* the family of God (Romans 8:29-30). Therefore, we

ARE righteous, the same as Abraham, the spiritual giant patriarch of the Hebrew people! It's a ***fact.*** But again, it's because of what God did for us - it is His gift - and certainly not because of what we do, feel or think.

We often don't perceive ourselves as being righteous (completely right with God), but as long as we have accepted Jesus into our lives, it is a fact that we are righteous, because GOD says it is true. And even more, as Christians, we have been born into royalty (1 Peter 2:9).

Although God *assures us* that we are righteous through Christ's payment for our sin, it doesn't mean that we always *act or feel* righteous. For this reason, we may even counter God and say "I am not righteous!" But when we say this, we are proving that we don't understand **what God has already accomplished for us**.

Of course, this doesn't mean we get to act any way we want and get His stamp of approval. There is a responsibility on our part to maintain our intimacy with Jesus and to obey His Word (John 14:15, 21a). Therefore, we must be careful not to abuse this gift; God says that we are sure to reap what we sow - to get back what we have given out - whether good or evil (Galatians 6:7-9).

The following Scriptures help explain why it is important to believe in faith, and then act on our position in Christ. The life goal of the Christian is to serve God by serving others. Our faith should inspire us to go out and lead others to Jesus and to make disciples for God's Kingdom, through the power of the Holy Spirit (Matthew 28:18-20). If we claim that we are identified with Jesus, but we don't bear any fruit - if there is no evidence of our faith - then our faith is *useless* (John 15:1-8; James 2:14-26; Hebrews 6:7-8)!

Faith Is Always *Dynamic*

The Greek word Dunamis is where we get our English word "dynamite and dynamic". It is also the same root word used for "the Power of the Holy Spirit - Dunamis Power" - which is translated as "miraculous power". Because the Holy Spirit lives inside of believers, we can relate this very power to our own faith. Our *dynamic*, indeed, *active* belief in God is not passive, but is always in motion, ever-changing, powerful, and ever-growing (or dying – *but never neutral*).

It is our faith that moves God to impart His Spirit, His grace, and His purposes into our lives, as well as the lives we touch for Christ. This doesn't mean that we have the power to make God do what we want! It doesn't mean that His grace is contingent on our actions - if we "do good enough", He is obliged to bless us. Nor does it mean that if we believe "hard enough", we will always get what we are praying for. It also doesn't guarantee that if we are on our "best behavior" or making right choices, that we will be free of pain or problems. We must realize that God is Sovereign, and He will choose the time and manner in which He answers our prayers of faith.

However, the Bible tells us that faith *is* a "Prime Mover" in the Kingdom of God (Hebrews 11:1-40). Again, as we believe God's Word (believing faith), it inspires us (active faith) to **work** in His Kingdom (Titus 3:4-8). Our faith should compel us to carry out the most important task at hand – which is to become a Dynamic Disciple of Jesus Christ *in order to reach the lost* (Romans 1:9).

There is no excuse for not sharing the Gospel with those whom God has placed in our lives! We *must* impact and influence others for Jesus. We may not be teachers or evangelists, but God gives us scores of opportunities each day to point people to Jesus. When we stand before Him, the thing that will matter the most is how we loved Him and brought souls to Him. There is a chapter in this book called *Sharing Our Faith* that will help you learn to do this.

Lastly, we need to be cautious of choosing only "positive" Scriptures and "claiming them as our own". While we are to cling to the promises of God, we need to take **the whole counsel** of Scripture into our hearts, which often speaks of the Refiner's Fire and the crucifixion of our own will, desires and plans. There is a balance between God's amazing love and His fierce anger towards sin! We must take love with justice, hardship with glory, and the Cross with the Crown (Romans 8:16-17; Philippians 1:29; 1 Peter 2:21).

Jesus, Our Freedom

In addition to our imputed righteousness, God also says:

2. We are Free....(Romans 6:5-11). The Bible says that we are slaves - either to righteousness (God), or to our flesh (sin and disobedience) (Romans 6:12-23). The truth is, if we reject Jesus Christ, we have no choice but to live in rebellion to God, which is sin (John 8:24; 16:9; Romans 5:12-19; 8:6-8). But with Jesus living inside of us through the power of the Holy Spirit, we are now free from the POWER of darkness, and liberated to serve God in ways that are wholesome, joyful, and eternal.

Christians have been set free by a process known as *redemption* (Hebrews 9:11-12). This word means "to buy back or to liberate". The concept of redeeming someone or something originated in the Old Testament. If a family member was in danger or in need, especially a widow, a male relative had the responsibility to help or rescue them. The title given to this "rescuer" is the *redeemer.* I just love that name! (Read Ruth, chapters 3 and 4). What is so incredible about this story is that Ruth became part of Jesus' bloodline. Jesus is now the Christian's Redeemer - delivering us from sin, fear of death, and eternal torment- because He paid the price to rescue us (Luke 1:68; Colossians 1:13-14).

Continuing along with this concept of being set free, we read in Isaiah 61:1 that one of Jesus' purposes in coming to earth was to set the captives free – into spiritual freedom. Mind you, this passage was written nearly 700 years before Jesus came to the earth, and we know now it is Jesus that Isaiah is prophesying about. We see this fulfilled in Luke 4:18-21, as Jesus reads the Scriptures about **Himself**. God and His Word are remarkable!

Similar to what we learned about our Righteousness in Christ, we certainly may not *feel or act* free after we have received salvation. We are still prone to hold onto and fall into those things that entangle us (Hebrews 12: 1-4).

However, we now have the *power* to resist sin. Before we accepted the Holy Spirit, we were unable to live to please God or to bring Him glory. That is because we are literally born into sin until we are regenerated by Jesus and His Spirit.

But God's heart has always been to have a people who are deeply in love with Him and committed to His plans. We see this displayed with His beloved Israelites nearly 1600 years before Christ (Exodus 8:1). And His heart has never changed! Jesus came to earth to pay for our sin, so we could be in full relationship with our holy God.

In this passage from Exodus, I find it interesting that God freed His people *so they could worship Him*. This is exactly the point of us being liberated from our sin today! "His people" are those who truly worship Him – by believing in Him, loving Him, following Him, and allowing Him to radically change their lives.

Another Legal Matter

Similar to the righteousness God has bestowed upon us as believers, our freedom in Christ is also a legal principle. As born again Christians, we have *already* been set free in the spiritual realm, because when Jesus died and rose again, He overpowered all the wicked forces. So, even though Satan is still the god of this world (2 Corinthians 4:4; Ephesians 2: 1-3), and he and his minions can certainly influence us, they no longer have *control* over us.

We now have the ability to *choose* holy living (1 John 4:4-6). This means that as we live IN CHRIST, we are more than conquerors, because our Master is the Great Conqueror (Romans 8:37). It's the same idea as an army that wins the war because their leader has navigated them through a victorious battle.

Again, God's way of freedom is the ability to choose to do the right thing, not the freedom to do whatever we feel like doing (Galatians 5:13; 1 Peter 2:16). We all have the capacity to sin - that's never difficult! We have all experienced the consequences of doing life "our way". But choosing right over wrong - the best over the mediocre - that takes God's mighty work in our lives.

Leaving Our Past Behind

An extremely important aspect of becoming free in Christ is our need to turn **away** from our old lives and turn **to** Jesus (Philippians 3:12-14).This is where so many people lose their way in the faith. They think that "not doing" certain things will bring them joy, peace, and right standing with God.

It cannot be overemphasized - we must realize that **being free in Christ isn't about keeping rules and following regulations**! That is RELIGION ☹. This is a common pitfall we may fall into while we are healing. "Religiosity" is basically trading our slavery to our past for slavery to our religion. If we only live "by the rules" without love and joy, people will not be attracted to Christ and His Spirit in us. We may go to church, read the Bible, and say "Christian things", but we need to be careful not to become "outward Christians" only.

Another obstacle to our freedom in Christ is when we have one foot firmly planted in the past while trying to live a new life in the present. This will never work! We must actively and fully move in a new direction of focus and obedience towards our Lord. However, this simply cannot be done without a supernatural change in our hearts and minds.

The secret to the Christian life is all about using our time and energy to fall in love with Jesus. Our job is to learn what He desires from us in the Bible. To spend time in prayer, talking with Him, asking Him for wisdom and direction, and then carrying out in obedience that which we have learned.

Furthermore, it is not enough to just "let go" of our past, but to *forcefully get rid of it* (Colossians 3:5-10)! This doesn't mean we pretend that bad things haven't happened to us, or we forget the pain that we may have caused others, and put on a fake smiley face. But we are to begin embracing Jesus' way of living instead of our old ways of relating.

For example, Jesus tells us that we must forgive the people who have harmed us and to restore relationships where possible. Otherwise, we will never truly be free from our past. This is where we often find that the old saying "forgive and forget" is not entirely true. We will never forget our old lives, but we certainly *can* forgive through God's power. I have had to forgive many people who did great harm to me, but I am free as a result.

It is this accumulation of past hardships and old patterns of thinking and behaving that we need to allow God to release from our lives. In fact, He tells us pointedly that unless we let go, we will not be fit for His Kingdom (Luke 9:62).

We can liken this Scripture to our lives. The "plow" can be seen as the life and work that God has planned for our future, and "looking back" is our past. While we may need to *consider* our past in order to heal, grieve, and give witness of where God has brought us from, we are not to <u>dwell</u> on it. God cannot use us if we defiantly refuse to forgive ourselves and those who have hurt us.

Indeed, if we *continue* to look backward instead of forward, we begin to look like the prisoner who has been told they can leave the prison, but they refuse to walk out the door! Or maybe you've heard of people who physically leave a prison, but soon after, they purposely do something to land them right back in. We call this "institutionalization".

This happens because they feel unsafe and uncomfortable without the strict rules and regulations of incarceration. Similarly, we become prisoners of our past when we refuse to let it go, often feeling "safer" in a familiar, but often unhealthy lifestyle. Moving ahead is frightening, but it is essential to boldly take steps forward if we want a new life.

<u>How Can I Get Past My Past?</u>

A healthy response to dealing with our past is to allow God to bring to our remembrance the things of which we need to repent and heal from. But this takes time, because we can't deal with the intensity of all of our failures and pain all at once. As He brings past situations and people to our attention, we need to face the thoughts and feelings head-on, and to weep over them if necessary.

We can begin this process of living out our freedom in Christ by learning how to grieve for the people, opportunities, and things we have lost. Again, we must take time to mourn over the ways we have been hurt and the way we have hurt others. We then need to *allow* God to heal us over time.

A word of caution: being able to heal from our past does not mean that we have to go over every single little thing that has happened in our lives! Ask God to bring the old experiences and situations to mind that *truly* need healing. And for those of you who have had a wonderful life, with little experience of hardship, pain, or broken relationships - be grateful for that! But the truth is, most of us have something we need to deal with from our past.

In my life, there was great healing in letting myself experience the pain I felt from my horrible childhood, all of the lost opportunities I'd missed, the wounds I had inflicted on others, and my own self-destructive behavior. Sometimes this grief was excruciating, which is a major reason I had avoided it for so many years.

It was a process for God and I to sort out my past, but going through this without drugs, avoidance, or blaming others actually helped me to move into my new life. It is essential to realize that just ignoring what sin has done to our lives and pretending we're all "new and happy" will cause us more problems.

<u>Let It Go!</u>

The next step to living in freedom is to quit bringing up that sin or offense which you have grieved! This is often where we end our pilgrimage in moving into our new life. We can really get "stuck" here if we choose to wallow in our self-pity and unhealthy patterns of thinking, feeling, and relating (Ephesians 2:1-10; Galatians 5:1).

Holding on to our past, not forgiving those who have hurt us, and choosing to be consumed with our old hurts and failures is ***disobedience,*** because Jesus died to give us NEW life and we must learn to walk in that gift (Romans 6:12-13; 2 Corinthians 5:15-17; Philippians 3:12-14).

Additionally, joy, peace, and love are strangled when we live in fear, anger, unforgiveness, or selfishness. Like any new experience, it takes time to develop our new skills. We can become fearful of being free. But this is how we begin to lay a new foundation for our future in Christ.

It takes great courage and effort to rebuild our lives! But the step to wholeness is *allowing* the Lord to heal us. The Bible - the very Word of God - has the power to cleanse, heal, comfort, convict, and direct us. We read the directive in Philippians 4:6-9 to fix our minds on things that are positive. This really means to dwell on Jesus, who embodies all of the characteristics listed in verse 8.

By the way, this is not “positive thinking”. It is called “renewing our minds” by the supernatural power of the Word of God (Romans 12:2; Hebrews 4:12). Part of moving ahead is purposefully keeping our eyes on the prize, which is our future in glory (Colossians 3:1-4; 2 Timothy 4:6-8)! Knowing that we will one day be with our Lord in perfect peace and love forever will give us hope for the future and help us through our earthly hardships (1 Corinthians 15:43; 2 Corinthians 4:17).

Lastly, even after we gain our freedom, there will be times when we may temporarily enslave ourselves to our old habits and thoughts again (2 Peter 2:19-22). The important thing is that we “get back up” - we repent and continue pressing on towards Christ. Continuing to stay close to the Lord will soon become our lifestyle, reaping its own reward. And when we face Jesus, we will have “fought the good fight” (1 Timothy 6:12). I desperately want to hear Him say to me “Well done, my good and faithful servant” (Matthew 25:21)!

CHAPTER 5

LAYING THE FOUNDATION

PART 2

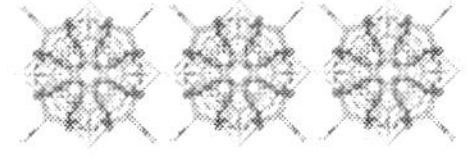

In Chapter 4, we read about several spiritual things that God completes for us through His Spirit once we accept Jesus into our lives. We now understand that God has made us righteous, which means that we are "right" in His sight. As born-again believers, this gives us the privilege of being able to come boldly into His presence through prayer, and to have an intimate relationship with Him (Hebrews 4:16).

We also learned that God has freed us from the control of sin. We certainly will not be "sinless" this side of heaven, but because Jesus lives inside of us through His Holy Spirit, we now have Gods' power and ability to *choose* His plan for our lives. This wonderful plan includes the ability to reject sin and carry out the design He has for each one of us to serve Him and further His Kingdom (Jeremiah 29:11; Titus 2:11-14). We really can experience *true* freedom!

In this chapter, we'll continue to explore what Christ has done for us, and learn about several other gifts He has imparted to us so that we can lay a sturdy and healthy foundation of faith. It will help us to understand our new position in Jesus.

3. God has also:

Seated us with Christ in the Heavenly Realms (Ephesians1:3, 19-20)

What in the world does that mean?

This is such a beautiful picture of our position in Christ. Because of Jesus' death, burial, and resurrection, He not only rescued us from spiritual death and eternal punishment, but He also conquered the powers of hell and the devil (Revelation 1:12-18). Jesus won the prize!

Even though we still see much evil in the world at this time, Satan will be overthrown and silenced forever when Jesus returns at His Second Coming (Revelation 20:10). And our blessed hope will finally be realized - we will be with our Lord forever.

The Bible tells us that 40 days after Jesus rose from the dead, He ascended back to heaven. There, God seated Him at His right hand (Luke 22:69; Hebrews 12:1-2). This means that when our lives are joined with His, *He literally places us with Himself in this heavenly domain* (Ephesians 2:4-6). This portrays our new identity in Christ.

Of course, we won't have the experience of knowing Him fully until we are with Him in eternity, but as His followers, our *spirits* are alive *with* Him and *in* Him right now (Ephesians 2:1-7)!

While this new nature begins at the moment of salvation, we will also continue to grow and mature in our knowledge and relationship with Christ throughout our lives (2 Corinthians 5:17; Philippians 1:9-11). This is what is referred to as being "in Christ".

The concept of "being seated" with Christ means that *we enter into a personal relationship with Almighty God Himself.* This is a mind-boggling privilege! We often take this relationship for granted, because we now live in an age of "grace". We may tend to think of Jesus as more of a friend than our Master and King.

Though He is both friend and Almighty God, we need to be careful to love and respect His entire character, not just the warm and fuzzy part. He still has the power to wipe out nations just by the command of His word (Revelation 19:15)! He is Perfect, altogether Holy, unimaginably Powerful, and deserving of our absolute adoration and devotion.

What a Privilege!

In order to appreciate what a special honor it is to have this intimacy with Jesus, it helps to understand how things were in the Old Testament. In biblical times, being allowed into someone's house (to "sit" with them) was a privilege. It meant you were friends, fully accepted and trusted. Eating a meal with others (called breaking bread) was very personal, as you sat face-to-face with them. Incidentally, the sacrament of communion alludes to this idea of God's family uniting to share a "meal" and to worship God together.

We can easily miss the depth of this type of relationship in our American culture today, because we often eat fast food as we drive to our destination, or we run out the door with a snack in our hand. We rarely eat at the table to talk and share with each other. But this habit regrettably robs us of intimate and personal time together.

To elaborate further on this idea, we must understand the honor and respect the Jewish people had for God. This reverence was so profound, they even developed an unwritten code in which they wouldn't even say the name "God", because they felt it was disrespectful.

So being *friends* with GOD was a truly countercultural idea in Jesus' time and was absolutely unthinkable (John15:14-15)! Sitting for a meal together with God would be an absurd idea! But Jesus, as the Great Mediator, has made a way so that we *can* come into God's presence (Revelation 3:20). We can now be **intensely** intimate with God the Father, God the Son, and God the Holy Spirit, because we are part of their family.

Additionally, the Bible tells us that "being seated in the heavenly realms" means that when we are *in* Christ, we are co-heirs to all that He has (Galatians 4:6-7; Ephesians 1:11; Romans 8:15-17). An heir is someone who receives the inheritance of the Father. Indeed, we will share a great legacy when we get to heaven!

God also says that we will *reign* with Him (2 Timothy 2:12; Revelation 20:6; 22:3-5). The word *reign* means "to rule", "to govern", "to control", "to lead", and "to administrate". That means we'll actually be running the place with Jesus ☺

Wait! There's More!

4. In Christ, we are **Justified**

I have heard the word "justified" explained as "Just as if we'd never done it". That's a pretty good description. And guess what? It's another legal term. It means "to make straight", "to make right", "to line up", or "to validate". For example, the Scripture says "He (the Lord) will make your paths straight" (Proverbs 3:5-6 NASB; parenthesis mine). So another way to say that might be "He will *justify* your paths (your life choices and direction).

Because of our sin nature, we have an innate (inborn) desire to justify *ourselves.* But in my thinking, self-justification = **excuses**. We will do anything to make others think that we are not at fault, or that we are not as bad as the situation might appear to make us. We constantly try to rationalize our actions - as if we'd never done it - or didn't do it as bad as it seems we did it!

NOT GUILTY!

The principle relating to justification began in the Old Testament. The Moral Law - which is The Ten Commandments - was essentially what "made one guilty" (Romans 7:7). The Law laid out the rules, and if you didn't live up to every one of them, you were a sinner – "GUILTY" (James 2:10-11).

That's why the Scripture says "For everyone has sinned; we all fall short of God's glorious standard" (Romans 3:23). Now we all know in our hearts that when we do something wrong, a "payment" is required. This actually began with Adam and Eve when they rebelled against God's authority. God took the first step to cover their sin by fashioning animal skins for them to hide their nakedness and shame. This implies that an animal had to have been slain – the first time in the Bible where sin was equated with death (Genesis 3:21).

Later in history, God devised a sacrificial system for His people. A perfect, spotless lamb, goat or bull was to be slaughtered for the sins of the nation (Leviticus 23:12). As mentioned in the last chapter, this was a word picture to show the Israelites how horrible sin was. A *life* needed to be taken for their sin (Leviticus 17:11).

The problem with our sin is that we are absolutely incapable of paying for it. No amount of work is sufficient to make up for our wrongdoing. We needed someone to rescue us. This is precisely why Jesus became the True Sacrifice for all of mankind, for all time.

Because He was perfect and sinless, He was just the right Offering that God required. In fact, that is why He is called "The Lamb of God" (John 1:29). He was the Sacrifice chosen to pay for our sin. Christ "fulfilled" the Law *for* us because only He lived without sin (Hebrews 9:24-26; 10:1-18).

It bears repeating - when we are *in Christ*, we are no longer "guilty" in God's eyes, because when Jesus died on the Cross, HE justified us. He paid our debt of sin - the punishment *we* deserved.

He "took our place". But again, only those who place their trust in Him are justified.

We are now made right with God - in alignment with Him and validated. This may be a difficult truth to accept because we know what we have done! But we must believe this truth, because *God says it to be true*. When God looks at the genuine, born-again believer, He sees Jesus - the Sacrificial and Righteous Payment.

The Passover

This sacrificial system is also portrayed in the "Passover" story that we've often heard of in the Bible. In the early history of their nation, the Israelites (who are also called Hebrews) were slaves in Egypt. God wanted His people freed, and He chose Moses to confront Pharaoh, the Egyptian leader, to demand the release of the Israelites. But Pharaoh would not listen to Moses' requests. God told His people that He was going to judge Pharaoh and his people for keeping the Israelites hostage.

After 9 devastating plagues, Pharaoh *still* refused to free the Hebrew people. The last (and worse) judgment was that God was going to kill every firstborn child and animal in the land.

In order to save His own people, God commanded the Israelites to sprinkle the blood of a lamb over the doorposts of their homes that night. The painted blood was the sign that God was to "pass over" the house and not bring death to that dwelling (Exodus 12:1-13, 23). Many Jews still celebrate this Passover memorial today in remembrance of being delivered from bondage in Egypt.

What is so fascinating is that since the death, burial, and resurrection of Christ, we as His followers have His shed blood "covering" us (Romans 5:9; Ephesians 1:7, 2:13; Hebrews 9:22). The "blood covering" in the Old

Testament was but a foreshadow of what our crucified Savior would do for us over a thousand years later.

Therefore, we have escaped judgment - IF we are authentically saved. We receive salvation by first admitting that we are sinners - realizing that a Holy God cannot tolerate our sin, and then determining to let Him lead us in a new life.

We must also have faith that God loved us enough to send His Son, Jesus, to rescue us by His redeeming blood (Romans 8:9; 1 Peter 1:2; 1 John 1:7; Revelation 1:5). Lastly, we believe that He was buried and rose from the dead. Jesus is now with the Father, and He will bring us to be with Him eternally at the appointed time (Romans 10:9; Ephesians 1:20).

Now it's important to realize that just because Jesus died for all of mankind, it is only those who choose to be in relationship with Him will gain these benefits. He is *available* to everyone. But unfortunately, not all will be saved, because this relationship needs to be purposefully entered into with all of our being (Mark 12:30; John 3:16-18).

Finally, while it is Jesus' blood that cleanses us, forgives us, and heals us spiritually, and although He performed this great feat *for* us, we still have the responsibility of nailing our ungodly passions to the Cross and crucifying them daily (Galatians 5:24-25).

All healthy relationships require both sides to work together towards a mutual goal, and it's no different in our relationship with the Lord. We are co-workers in His purposes and plans. And the amazing byproduct of His gift of righteousness and justification is that we are given the ability to overcome our fleshly (sin) nature (Colossians 2:11-15).

Authentic Salvation

Another reason why we are incapable of justifying ourselves before a Holy God is because only *He* can make us right with *Himself* - for He is the only true Judge (Romans 3:24-25b). It is vital to understand that justification is the work of God alone. We are completely powerless to make ourselves right with Him!

However, just because we are forgiven and justified, this doesn't mean that God doesn't 'really see' our sin. Or that our sin does not matter. Quite the contrary, our sin can completely ruin our relationship with God. Some people believe in the concept of "Once saved, always saved" – in other words, "now that I'm saved, I've got a free ticket and can live any way I want and nothing I ever do will take that away".....

But if we casually 'accept' Jesus at one time and then live our lives against His Word, His ways, and His principles continuously - essentially rejecting Him completely - then we have to seriously consider if we were ever redeemed in the first place (Hebrews10:26-39; 1 John 2:1-6; 15-17; 20-29).

Someone who is genuinely saved and has a relationship with Christ cannot help but exhibit a different lifestyle. You may wonder why I keep using the words "genuinely and authentically" saved. This is because many people mistakenly think they are going to heaven for a variety of reasons (I'm a good person; God loves me and would never judge me; I don't believe in hell...)

But the Bible is clear that there is only ONE way to heaven, and that is through Jesus Christ (John 14:6). While this may sound "narrow minded", it's the truth.

Think of it this way: Let's say you're driving into a new town. You ask someone for directions. They say "Go down this road for a mile and turn right. It's a one way street, so don't miss it". If you decide to turn left at that intersection, you will be lost. Is that narrow-minded? No! It's a fact and it's up to *you* to follow instructions!

Additionally, our lives should look different after we're saved. We don't become absolutely "perfect", but growing into the likeness of our Savior is part of the proof that we have received new life. Jesus enables us to live a life of vitality. He changes our morals and attitudes. He then gives us the power and compassion to offer His salvation and discipleship to those who don't know Him.

It's been said that "the Christian life is simple, but not easy". How true! Jesus explained that the 10 commandments are now fulfilled in just 2 precepts, called the "Royal Law" (Mark 12:30-31; Romans 13:8-10; James 2:8). If we really live according to God's Word and principles, and love Him and others deeply, we will naturally obey the Law. Loving God and loving others is a lifestyle of sacrifice. We won't *want* to kill, envy, or steal.

We won't want to hurt God, ourselves, or anyone else. But this, of course, is only accomplished by living under the power of the Holy Spirit.

5. In Christ, we are **Sanctified**

The word 'sanctify' means "to set apart", "to appoint", "to purify", or "to dedicate". The Bible says that we are *sanctified* as believers. It might be easier to understand sanctification by thinking of the word "holy", because they are often used interchangeably in our faith. This means that at the moment of our salvation, ***God*** *makes us holy*. And when we enter into this relationship with Him, we ARE set apart from the world for His good plans and pleasure.

Hearing that we are "holy" may make us revolt inwardly as we say "I am *not holy*! Only God is holy!" But the Bible makes it clear that we, as Christ's followers, are an altogether separate and different people group. *Jesus* has *made* us holy by His sacrifice; it is not by our desire (John 17:9-19; 1 Corinthians 1:2, 30-31; 6:11; Colossians 1:21-23; 1 Thessalonians 5:23-24; 1 Peter1:2-4)! And we are to represent Christ according to this Truth.

Digging deeper, we find that *sanctification* has two aspects. One aspect is that our spirits are *immediately* sanctified when we receive Jesus into our hearts. Before salvation, our spirits were dead, but they have now been "made alive" in Christ (Colossians 2:13; Titus 3:4-5).

This is why the Bible refers to our salvation as "rebirth", "born again" and "created anew". For this reason, we can commune with the living God at the very moment we accept Christ. He gives us His mind and His Spirit right then. We are literally made holy enough to house His Holy Spirit.

The other side of sanctification is that our "flesh" still needs work!

Hebrews10:14 talks about this two-part sanctification. It says "For by that one offering He (Christ) forever made perfect those who are being made holy". So, the "*forever made perfect*" part of this Scripture is that we ARE holy and perfect in His eyes at conversion.

The last part of this Scripture verse that says "*those who are **being made** holy*" is where our old sin nature is *continuing* to be changed and purified, day by day. This happens through prayer, as well as through the cleansing we receive from reading, studying, and obeying the truth of the Bible. We are also made holy through serving God, and disciplining ourselves in His ways (2 Peter 1:10).

So far, we have learned much about our position in Jesus. In the next section, we will learn more about the important part that we play in this tremendous relationship with our Lord.

6. Our **responsibility as Christians**

It has already been mentioned that there is a two-sided aspect to our relationship with God. We find that many of the promises in the Bible are contingent (dependent) upon our response to the Lord and His Word. We are given amazing gifts by God, but we must strive to live close to Him and obey Him. It is only then that we will live **successfully** in the positional truths we have been learning about.

While our salvation is free - no strings attached - it cost Jesus Christ His own life. And the remainder of our relationship-including our level of intimacy with Him, the depth of our commitment to Him, the effectiveness of the fruit of His Spirit in us, and the ability to reach the lost - is directly related to how we live up to *our* part of the 'bargain'.

Being a Christian is not just in name only. It's a ***lifestyle,*** not just "saying" that we believe (James 2:19-20). *Belief* is intimately intertwined in the way we think, talk, and behave. Remember, James says that "Faith without good deeds is useless". The truth is, a life that is immersed in Jesus can't help but be dynamic and overflow to others!

How Can We Know if We are Growing?

If we are new to the Christian faith, one way we can tell if we are becoming more like Jesus is that we will begin to lose interest in some of the things we used to do. The previous friends and associates we spent time with who live apart from Jesus will begin to seem foreign. We will have a new awareness between right, wrong, and mediocre living. As we move further into this relationship, we will start to crave the things of God and refrain from things we used to think were permissible to do.

However, you must take heed! You will most likely start to have resistance from people in your life; at work, school, and home! Others will not understand why you are changing. They may even become angry, because you are altering the comfortable or familiar relationship they had with you.

At this point, you will need to prayerfully consider whether your friendship is worth keeping. Oftentimes, we'll find that the people we "thought" were our friends are not really our friends at all. A true friend will always want the best for you. On the other hand, there are times when God may give you opportunities to lovingly share your faith with them.

As we continue in our relationship with Christ, we'll be able to see other landmarks that we are growing. Just as a tree matures, we can measure the health of our spirituality by the "fruit" in our lives. Our thoughts, behavior, and motives will begin to change as we become more like Jesus (Luke 6:43-44).

Examining ourselves regularly to see if we are manifesting the Spirit's attributes as outlined in Galatians 5:22-24 is a necessary practice. We should take inventory of what we believe and how it is affecting our walk with Christ. It's easy to get sidelined and have our prayers and our focus only on ourselves. Looking out *from* our own lives to help strengthen, support and pray *for others* will be a sign of growth, and it will bring us great joy and much glory to God!

Our Commitment

A. We are *commanded* to live righteously, in holiness and purity (2 Timothy 2:21-22). We all know that we can't do this without help! Praise God that that He supplies the "help" we need by the Holy Spirit living within us. It is when we resist the Spirit's power and guidance in our Christian walk that we will ultimately fail. And most likely, we will not draw others to our beautiful Savior (Galatians 5:16-21).

The fact is, when we use our own strength and intelligence to further our plans **apart from** God, we reap a "fleshly" harvest. This way of life has a natural progression; it begins with our thoughts and desires, and advances into our human planning and arranging.

Ultimately, we find that the outcome of this behavior is unhealthy and unlovely (Galatians 6:8). When we want what *we* want, and not really what God wants, we become "Christians" who don't act much like our Lord. This is what is meant by the term *carnal Christians* (James 4:8; 1 Peter 4:2-3).

Now this certainly doesn't mean we are to live in a "super-spiritual" world and do nothing. Or that God will take care of us without any effort on our part, if we only pray hard enough! Quite the contrary, we are to use our minds, strength, time and finances to live a productive life on earth. I'm talking about planning our lives without *any* input from the Lord.

Perhaps you'll say that there are many people – even unbelievers (people who don't love or follow Jesus) - who do "good" things for the world. They may use their own creativity and ingenuity to accomplish things, and they aren't considered "evil". Well, that may be true. But when we do things apart from God's power and design, no **eternal** "fruit" is produced from our labors.

Also, think of the majority of the results of mankind's efforts. When we do "good deeds" without God's direction, we are apt to become proud of our accomplishments. We often become greedy when money is involved. We don't want to share the spotlight when we are rewarded for our abilities. We tend to become obsessed with achieving greater, more, and better. Even if this doesn't sound like you personally, the reality is that when we feed our flesh, our base desires usually end up controlling us (Romans 6:16; 2 Peter 2:19).

B. We are to <u>flee</u> from sin (Romans 6:12-23). That means to RUN from it like you would a burning forest! We so often want to *live* with sin, instead of running from it. We make poor choices to play with sin, and when the consequences come due, we want to blame the world, our circumstances, other people, and the devil for it.

While the world, circumstances, other people and the devil DO influence our behavior, the Bible says that our FLESH is what makes us sin –and it is absolutely *our* responsibility to reject it (Romans 8:12-13; James 1:14-15)!

In the meantime, even if we do sin *occasionally* - not as a lifestyle - we have the great comfort that Jesus will restore us **as** we repent (that means to *really* turn away from our sin and fix our gaze on

Jesus, not just mouth empty promises and keep doing the same old thing) (2 Corinthians 7:10; 1 John 1:9).

As we can all attest, sin really does birth feelings of inadequacy, frustration, guilt, fear, and resentment in our lives. Furthermore, it creates hopelessness in becoming like Christ. It only keeps us in bondage.

A prolonged life of sin results in a lack of JOY and PEACE. And ultimately, if we purposefully continue to reject Christ, His Word, His people, and His ways, it can certainly lead to spiritual death (Romans 8:5-8; Galatians 6:7-10; Hebrews 6:4-6).

C. We are to determine what pleases the Lord (Romans 14:17-19; Ephesians 5:10; 1Thessalonians 5:18).

Colossians 1:9-10 shows us several ways that we can please the Lord:

- prayer
- gain knowledge of His will and understanding
- receive His spiritual wisdom
- make time to gain biblical and godly understanding
- produce good (godly and eternal) fruit
- learn to grow in our faith
- make an effort to get to know God more intimately

It is essential that we *feed* on Jesus **daily**. That means taking control of our time and desires. We must spend time in Bible study, prayer, and meditation in order to know Him more intimately.

Also, becoming involved in a Bible-believing and obeying Church body, and spending time with Christians who deliberately live for Jesus and exhibit His character in their lives will help us to *successfully* accomplish this instruction from our Lord (Proverbs 3:5-6; Romans 12:1-2).

We are to ***put off*** wickedness and ***throw off*** our old nature
We are to ***let*** the Holy Spirit renew our thoughts and attitudes
We are to ***put on*** the new nature (Ephesians 4:17-24)

While God does the majority of the "work" in our lives by offering us salvation and bringing us into the fullness of maturity in our faith, we are called to put our best effort forward to remain close to Him and to obey what He asks of us.

It's not about the rules and regulations! It's about the *relationship*! Remember, the more intimate we become with Jesus, the less likely we are going to want to hurt Him, to disregard Him, or to rebel against Him. This is what will give us the strength and the power to obey Him!

As our reward, He will begin to change our hearts and minds as we live in Him, so that our desires line up with His. It's a remarkable and supernatural progression of faith, and it IS life-changing!

As we put forth the effort to be godly, the Lord will enable us and strengthen us. And we will continue to grow from "glory to glory" (2 Corinthians 3:15-18). The following is a list of character traits we should begin to exhibit in growing measure as Jesus shines from our lives (Philippians 1:9-11).

- Love
- Be kindhearted
- Grow in the faith
- Pray without ceasing
- Forgive quickly and easily
- Make every effort to stay in the Spirit
- Be patient with one another
- Read the Word regularly, prayerfully, and thoughtfully
- Think about Heaven!
- Make peace whenever possible
- Do not bring sorrow to God's Spirit by the way you live
- Be thankful in *everything*
- Rejoice constantly!
- Serve whenever you have the opportunity

I challenge you to pick one of these attitudes/actions a week and DO them!

When we work in tandem with the Lord, miraculous transformation takes place!

CHAPTERS 4 AND 5
LAYING THE FOUNDATION
REFLECTION

1. **What are the 5 spiritual positions that God has accomplished for you?**

____

____

____

____

____

2. **What are 2 essential "weapons" we need in order to be in God's service?**

____

____

____

____

____

3. **Do you think you are "cruising" or "battling" in your Christian walk right now? Why?**

____

____

____

____

____

4. **Do you feel secure in your relationship with Jesus? Or do you feel that you must continually strive to gain His favor and His love?**

   Do you often feel guilty?

   Or do you feel free to come to Him for everything?

   Do you feel special and loved?

5. **If you do not feel secure and loved in this relationship, would you be willing to start believing that God's truth about you is real? (i.e. you are loved, forgiven, treasured, equipped for service?)**

CHAPTER 6

SURRENDER

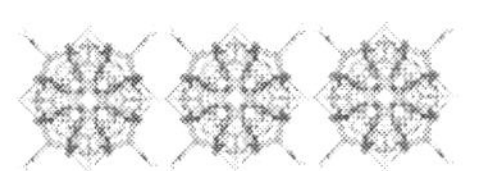

Many times when we hear the word 'surrender', we think of negative images. We might think of a country surrendering, thus making it weak. Maybe a child's game comes to mind where the one to surrender has lost to the 'competition'. Or possibly, you think of a criminal who surrenders to the police.

The word actually does mean 'to declare yourself defeated', or 'to relinquish possession or control of something because of coercion or force'. However, we are going to discover that biblical surrender results in a life of peace and purpose.

In our world today, we find little evidence of the act of surrender. Money is our god, and greed is ruthless. In the corporate world, to surrender is to fail. The 'almighty dollar' has surpassed people in importance. Often, we as Americans live 'only for ourselves', and giving up our time or resources to help others seems like a foreign concept. Not only that, we lack compassion and patience for those who do not live up to our expectations, or who cannot fulfill our needs.

God Desires Our Surrender

When God calls for our surrender, what He really wants is for us to *yield* to Him in an act of *willing* submission. This is an entirely different dynamic than the world's version of surrender. First, it is our *choice*. We purposefully turn over our rights as individuals, so that we can serve a higher purpose. Again, this does not mean we lose our identity - because

God actually *created* our uniqueness for His plans. As we come under His authority and leading, our destiny in this life becomes evident.

Another word for surrender is *submit*. The first step we take in our relationship with Christ is choosing to give up our old life for the life that He offers. This involves the act of *submission*. Just like the word surrender, it may bring thoughts of horror to some people's minds. They think of having to do what someone else wants, something that is completely against their desires.

Maybe you were in an abusive relationship and you vow you will never again submit to another person. Or you might have experienced a controlling, manipulative family member and feel terrified to think of turning your will over to anyone but yourself. Whatever the case, submission is a difficult concept to teach in the biblical sense, because so many people fear being subjugated to another. And we also have to deal with our own strong wills!

The biblical term for submission means 'to accept someone else's authority or will', or 'to defer to another's knowledge, judgment, or experience'. It involves turning our will over to God. It is similar to the secular definition, but the major difference is that when we submit to God, we are willingly placing ourselves into the hands of the One Who created us, Who loves us intensely, and Who always has our best interest at heart.

He is not out to manipulate us, overpower us, or take advantage of us. His main purpose is to fill us with His Holy Spirit, so that we can live a life that reflects His beauty and His glory. The benefits of turning our wills over to our Father far outweigh the disadvantage of living life only for ourselves.

God offers us a free choice to accept Him, obey Him, to worship Him and to love Him (or not). He will never force us to submit. But we need to be aware that there are consequences for us if we do not come under His authority.

We may not realize it, but we submit to circumstances and people all the time. This is usually a choice we make, such as obeying traffic regulations. Or, when we 'submit' to our boss, we may do things we don't want to do, such as working later hours than we had signed up for. In this sense, we decide to bend our will (submit) in order to keep the job, because losing the job may be worse than agreeing to do things we really don't want to do.

<u>Do You Have An Appetite?</u>

Part of submission has to do with controlling our 'appetites' with His help. This doesn't refer to the food we eat (although gluttony *is* overeating to the point of treating our bodies detrimentally). Our 'appetite' in biblical terms is also called our 'flesh'. This is the seat of our souls - our emotions, wills, and thoughts. We also refer to it as our passions.

God wants us to love Him with all of our hearts, minds, souls, and strength (Deuteronomy 6:5-9). He could have made robots, but He wanted to have a deep *relationship* with mankind in a mutually loving union, where both sides were devoted to each other because they *wanted* to be. He desires that our passion is for *Him*, as His is for us.

And that's why the apostle Paul talks about controlling our flesh, our passions. When we have sin as the 'default' mode in our lives, we naturally veer away from the Lord (Romans 8:5-8). But when we allow His Spirit to control us, then we bend towards God and His ways (Romans 8:9-14). It is His grace that allows this to happen (Romans 6:12-18).

<u>You Just Don't Understand!</u>

People who have not turned their lives over to the Lord have no idea what they are missing. It can be likened to a story about a fisherman who arrived to shore from his very first journey at sea. When he steps off of his boat, the crowd on the shore asks him how his voyage went, and he responds "It was terrible! The seas were rough and dangerous. It was cold and wet. And I was seasick almost the whole time!" The crowd, therefore, believes that this is what they will experience when traveling by sea.

Yet the next week, a cruise ship comes into town. Again, the crowd asks the voyagers what their trip was like. And they respond "It was gorgeous! We had the best food ever. The sun was shining, and we saw all different kinds of sea animals. It was so relaxing. We can't wait to go again!"

You see, the fisherman only saw one side of the story - his. Because of his limited knowledge and experience, he wasn't in the position to tell others what a wonderful experience they *could* have had, because he had never seen the beauty or felt the excitement that the cruise ship travelers had. And even though he *thought* he understood the whole truth, the complete picture was not revealed to him.

The very same principle applies to people who have not surrendered their lives to Jesus Christ. They have never experienced the loving, guiding, powerful, and protecting hand of God, so their knowledge is very limited. They think that a life of submission to the Lord will be boring. They assume it will lack fun and passion. Or that it will just be a long list of rules and regulations.

Many people 'think' they know God, and may even claim that they have 'read' the Bible. But 1 Corinthians 2:10-16 makes it plain that we **must** be indwelt by the Holy Spirit in order to understand the deep thoughts of God. Incidentally, the word 'spiritual' in this Scripture is not referring to the worlds' idea of spiritual.

Today, many people say they are spiritual, but they have no relationship with Jesus or God's Holy Spirit (John 14:6). They practice the worship of many gods, and believe that God is 'in' everyone and everything; that God 'loves and tolerates anything'; and that He would 'never send anyone to hell'.

They are deceived, and they live in darkness (1 Corinthians 1:18-25). They *refuse* to believe the truth. In reality, God has many facets to His personality. They include justice with mercy. And love as well as hatred for sin. He is a Giver, but requires our submission. Indeed, people send *themselves* to hell by choosing to reject Jesus (John 3:16-18; 16:9). God desires their fellowship now and their eternal companionship in heaven. He never wants **anyone** to go to hell. Nonetheless, only the human heart can reject the work of God (Luke 19:10).

To be even more direct, Jesus says that those who reject Him – those who do not love Him and accept His Spirit - are literally *of the devil* (John 8:42-46)! Now before you write that statement off as being narrow minded or intolerant, we need to remember that Jesus also made it clear that there are only two sides in the universe– His and Satan's (Matthew 12:30).

Christians aren't making this stuff up! They are not being uptight – they are only quoting what GOD has already said. There is no middle ground. This idea even applies to Christians who have never truly submitted their hearts, minds, and wills to Christ. They desperately hold on to old mindsets and attitudes, refusing to completely surrender. You can see this type of un-submissive behavior clearly, because their lives do not exhibit the fruit of the Holy Spirit, which is love, joy, peace, patience, kindness, gentleness, goodness, faithfulness, and self-control. Their 'walk' doesn't measure up to their 'talk'.

Now I'm not talking about those who love the Lord and are working on their issues by allowing His Spirit to change them. The fact is, while we still have breath, we will *always* struggle with our flesh (Romans 7:21-25). But as we continue seeking and submitting to Jesus, He promises to change the desires of our hearts (Psalm 37:3-5). Our lives should be in the process of transforming and reflecting more of His character over time. And we need to examine ourselves periodically to make sure this is happening.

<u>You *WILL*!</u>

As mentioned previously, we in our "individualistic" culture have a hard time surrendering our "freedom" to others. Indeed, there are circumstances in which we join (or are forced into) a 'cause', thereby losing some or all of our individuality. Think about a war, a religious cult, or a gang. Individuality is denied or suppressed in order to bring 'unity' to the whole. It's almost as if one needs to give up their entire personality so that the 'leader' is the only one being obeyed or elevated.

The interesting thing about Christianity is that it is full of 'oxymorons', which means "a statement that seems to contradict itself, but is, in fact, true". A few examples are: we are to 'die' to 'live'; we are to become humble to be great; and we are to sacrifice (our *selfishness* - not our personality) in order to bring unity. Following Jesus means loving Him with all of our hearts, minds, and strength.

Then there are other world religions that teach an 'emptying of your mind' in order to become 'one with the universe'. This is absolutely unbiblical. God wants our minds to be fully engaged when we think of Him and talk to Him!

Unlike the religious groups that deny its members individuality, God uses our unique talents and strengths to accomplish His will. As Christ is expressed through our lives, it brings out the true dimensions of the 'whole' - which is the Church - the Body of Christ.

Our behavior is often the only picture the world will ever see of Jesus. And that is why it is so essential to be a true representative of Him in our lives. Remember, our submission to Jesus is only beneficial if it is genuine (Matthew 23:25-27). People who aren't Christians know instinctively if we are authentic or not!

Don't Worry – God Doesn't Want Your Firstborn...☺

Sacrifice...Now there's a word we hate to hear!

When our lives become truly submitted to Christ, we will naturally start to sacrifice our time, talent, and money to further the kingdom of God. When Jesus is on the Throne in our lives, His ways become our ways. Since He is a Giver, a Lover, and the One Who made the Ultimate Sacrifice, we, too, should begin to act in this way. Actually, how we treat other people is one way to tell if Jesus *really* lives and rules in our lives.

Some of the ways we 'sacrifice' is to let go of our "right" to stand for an opinion we hold when it is in direct opposition to God's Word. Maybe we need to turn over our 'right' to continue in our sinful behavior. Perhaps it is our perceived 'right' to harbor resentments, unforgiveness, or self-righteous attitudes.

We were bought with the price of Jesus' blood, and as such, we should be honoring Him by allowing our lives to be changed for His glory (1 Peter 1:18-20). Our surrender will truly bring the most magnificent rewards.

How Does Submission Help My Life?

One of the most beautiful rewards of becoming a Christian is that we become part of a new family. We also become heirs to God's throne (Galatians 3:29; Romans 8:17). And we will receive all of the promises that God gives to Christ because we are now born into His lineage.

2 Chronicles 7:14-16 tells us that we are *called by His Name!* In the Old Testament, that was a huge honor. In biblical times, your name was associated with your character, and to be associated with someone whose name was respected meant that you, too, were in good standing.

The truth is that if we have genuinely accepted Christ and are willing to come under His authority, we are children of the King (1 Peter 1:3-5)! We are *royalty*. We are priests of the Most High God (1 Peter 2:5, 9)! We are friends and the beloved of the Master of the Universe! Truly, that's better than knowing any celebrity or earthly person we consider 'important'!

There is great blessing, but also great responsibility when we commit our lives to Christ. The above Scripture in second Chronicles also talks about humility, prayer, seeking God's face, and turning from our wicked ways – in order to have God hear us, forgive us, and heal our land (this encompasses our lives and our nation).

Submitting ourselves to the Lord is an essential component to receiving His blessings

Submitting to the Lord means to obey God <u>first</u>. It means to yield our bodies, minds, wills, emotions, spirits, finances, possessions, relationships, fears, and hopes, to Him. The Bible says that we are to "take up our cross and follow Jesus" (Matthew 10:38-39). This is a decision to relinquish our old ways and begin to let Him change the way we think and act. If we want our lives healed and we desire to have God hear our prayers - and if we want His promised blessings - then we need to follow the instruction of Scripture.

2 Chronicles 30:6-9 shows us some of God's directives, as well as the benefits of our surrender:

Directives	**Benefits**
Return to the Lord	He will return to us
Don't act like heathens	We won't become objects of derision (mockery)
Don't be stubborn	If we submit, then we will be treated mercifully

Submit ourselves to God	He will not continue to turn His face from us
Come into His Temple	We will be able to return to this land (be at home and at peace with God)
Worship Him	And His anger will be turned away *

**We need to remember that in the Old Testament, Jesus had not yet come. There was greater judgment then, because God's anger had not yet been 'satisfied' until Jesus' took our punishment upon Himself, by His death on the Cross. That's why we hear so much about God's anger and His turning away from people because of their sin in those times.*

But be aware that even today, those who reject Christ are still under condemnation. He is a Holy God and cannot be in the presence of sin. God's anger is still burning hot towards those who refuse to accept Him into their lives (Revelation 14:9-12). In this Scripture, we see that hell is real. You can see the contrast of those who believe in Jesus, and those who take the mark of the beast (unbelievers).

God is patiently waiting for this end-time event, though, because He surely does not want anyone to perish (2 Peter 3:9). As I've mentioned before, the awesome Gospel news is that when Jesus' blood covers our lives, God sees only the blood covering. Therefore, He can come near to us because we have been made holy and blameless (Colossians 1:22).

Because of the Cross, we now live in an era of grace and mercy. Now this doesn't mean we can act any old way we want and still have the Lord's blessings; many of the Old Testament principles are eternal and remain in effect today.

How Can I Learn to Submit to God?

When we *desire* the Lord, the Holy Spirit guides, changes, and renews us. We begin to actually die to our selfish stubbornness, thus becoming more pliable in God's hands. Submission means being willingly to come under God's discipline and direction. This means that we actively try to learn what He wants to teach us by listening and obeying. Here are some pointers as you choose to yield to God for His will in your life:

1. Silently reflect on what He wants for you and from you. This is accomplished through the reading and obeying of His Word, and prayer. Everything God desires and requires of us is in the Bible. There is no mystery!
2. Acknowledge His authority and choose to turn from your wicked acts. This is done as we repent and humble ourselves, which can only be done with His help. He is more than willing to give us the power to do His will! Philippians 2:13 says "For God is working in you, giving you the *desire* to obey Him and the *power* to do what pleases Him".

   Many Christians fail in obeying God because they are trying so hard 'to do the right thing', and they become discouraged when they can't. They end up thinking Christianity doesn't 'work'. What we need to do is rely on the Holy Spirit to empower us. Our job is to get closer to the Lord and to make choices that honor God.

Often, it is in the 'deciding' to honor Him that brings us the power to do so!

3. Exhibit self-control in our lives. This is one of the fruits of the Holy Spirit. Thank God that *we are not called to change our sin by willpower!* It helps to remember that God WANTS us to succeed in doing His will even more than we do! We aren't alone. While we do need to *choose* to listen and obey, God will continue to change us as we depend on Him and ask for His help in every situation.
4. Develop confident patience as we depend on our Lord to bring about the necessary changes in our lives, knowing that it will take time.

Jesus wants us to be excited about our decision to follow Him, but He also warns those who have superficial faith to either become more committed to Him, or to turn away altogether (Revelation 3:16-17). We see in these verses that when we are lukewarm, we are, in fact, spiritually blind. Therefore, we fail to realize how bleak our situation really is. A half-hearted follower is useless to God (John 15:6; 2 Peter 1:3-9).

Before we decide to follow Christ, we must 'count the cost', as a builder would *before* he builds the house. If he is inaccurate in his estimation, the building may end up only partially built. Just think - a half-built house is open to rain and wind, insects, and thieves. This is exactly how our lives are when we are only 'partially' committed to Christ.

Obviously, when we enter into salvation with the Lord, we won't begin to understand what lies ahead. But we must go in with our eyes open. Being a follower of Christ means *giving our lives away for Him no matter what the cost.* **God ordained our submission to prevent chaos**. Even Jesus submitted to the Father. Since Jesus is God and *He* submitted, we need to look closely at our own attitudes about this essential component to Christian living.

And don't be surprised - what may result from your choice to genuinely follow Jesus may include loss of social status, friends, or family. It means giving Him control of your money, time, and talent. You may be hated, made fun of, or separated from your loved ones. Ultimately, as in many countries today, you might even be tortured or put to death.

Are you SURE you still want to follow Jesus???!!! ☺

Lamentations 3:25-28 has some further wisdom for us:

Wait for God,
Seek God,
Come under the yoke of His discipline.

As we accept His authority, it is important to learn how to 'rest' in Him. We need to train ourselves to be quiet and meditate on His Word. It will mean a change in our old behavior to learn to 'wait' for Him. We must 'trust' in Him, and find ways to seek His opinion, His wisdom, and His ways. This means that we do not run ahead. When we pray about a decision, we don't go off immediately and do things the way we 'think' we should do them.

If we are uncertain about something that we've prayed about, we STOP. And we don't move ahead until we get the 'go ahead' from the Lord. We might also need to ask for godly counsel from trusted Christian friends. We often ask for advice from people who do not have the Holy Spirit living in them, which may seem like a good idea at the time, but most likely, it won't be God's advice.

It goes without saying that this concept does not pertain to our sin. There should be no need to 'pray' about our sinful behavior - if we are sinning, we need to stop. But if we are truly willing to have God's plan unfold in our lives, and if we genuinely desire His wisdom, then the process is to wait, seek, and submit.

I repeatedly say - Read God's Word! This cannot be overemphasized! Look for Him to speak to you through it. Using a Bible dictionary or concordance, you can look up Scriptures that apply to what you're going through, and see how others in the Bible handled their situation. Guard against taking phrases out of Scripture just to back up your own opinions. Pray deeply and continually about your problems and struggles.

God *will* speak to you if your heart is willing to hear the Truth. Pray for strength during your trial or temptation. Write your prayer requests down so you can later see God's answers. Pray for the desire to actually *do* what He tells you to do. Pray for a hedge of protection from Satan during this vulnerable time of testing or decision.

Remember, *the only person we can control is ourselves*. It is not our job to control others, but to let ourselves come under the authority of God in every area of our lives. Our mission as a Christian is to share Jesus with others and to live a life that stands out as a pure example of our Lord's control in our lives.

One word of caution: if we are living a 'Christian life' but not positively representing the Lord, then we need to be careful when we share our faith with others. If you are living an ungodly life only for yourself, then you look like a hypocrite to unbelievers. This is one very good reason why the unsaved dislike God and the church.

Secondly, you lead others to believe that being a Christian is easy – they can live contrary to God and still get to heaven. This is a discredit to God's name and character. We are not perfect, for sure, but being called by His name carries a price, and that price is submission and sacrifice.

Christian maturity means:

- making Christ the CENTER of our lives
- having genuine and intimate communion with Jesus -not depending on religious ritual
- not falling back into sin (or refusing to give up our sin)
- not trusting in ourselves, and
- not letting ANYTHING come between us and Christ.

Our job as Jesus' followers is to make sure that we receive what we need from Him. No human being will ever be able to give us the power to act like our Lord. No other person will be able to heal the deep recesses of our pain or our past. And likely, there are few people who will give themselves unconditionally to help us succeed.

But we can be transformed into the kind of people God desires – those who look out for each other, who love regardless of circumstances, and who bring unity to situations by prayer and self-sacrifice. This can be achieved by clinging to Jesus and receiving HIS power, His love, and His purpose for our lives. This is the only way this world will be healed, and it's certainly the only way that Christ's Church will be able to become what Jesus wants it to be.

It Really IS Wonderful!

In contrast to what we gain from the world's system, we receive entirely different benefits when we choose to surrender to God. Instead of getting money or power, our character is transformed. We acquire a brand new outlook on this life, and of the world to come. The joys of submission are too numerous to count. We begin to develop an intimate relationship with the Father, Son, and Holy Spirit. We receive real power over our sin and selfishness, because God's power now works through us.

As we continue to yield to His ways, we will start to bear sweet fruit. The things that caused us to live in fear, guilt and shame are erased – and in its place is a profound sense of self-esteem, a passion for life, a joy that surpasses the glitter of this world, and a sense that we are safe and secure, even in the midst of turmoil. What an exchange!

It's time to take an account of your life. What we have learned through this lesson has both immediate and long term benefits. Conversely, there are grave consequences for rejecting Jesus, or pretending to be a Christian, and yet not submitting to God's direction.

Jesus wants your **entire** life at His disposal. This is not something to be afraid of - instead, it is the true path to success and happiness! Begin today by asking Him to reveal the real condition of your relationship with Him. And ask Him for the power to fully submit your life to Him.

CHAPTER 6
SURRENDER
REFLECTION

<u>Worksheet</u>

Answering these tough questions can help you determine the course of your life:

1. **Are you afraid of truly surrendering your life to God? Write out how you feel about giving God:**

   <u>Your time</u>

   How much time do you spend helping others? Giving time to your church or the needy, etc?

   ____

   ____

   <u>Your thought life</u>

   How much time do you spend reading the Bible?

   ____

   Praising God?

   ____

   Praying?

   ____

   Thinking about Jesus throughout your day?

   ____

   <u>Your heart</u>

   Do you feel a strong passion about Jesus, or is He sort of on the 'back burner' in your life?

   ____

   ____

Do you love to meet with God, talk to Him, and read about Him in the Bible?

___

If you feel emotionally dry, would you be willing to pray for new passion for Him?

___

Your talent

What are your talents? And how often do you use them for advancing the Kingdom of God?

___

___

___

Your money

Do you tithe? (Give part of your money back to God at church)

___

What are your fears about giving your money to God?

___

___

Do you feel that your money will be misused if you give it to your church?

___

Do you think that you cannot 'afford' to regularly give some of your money to God?

___

Do you feel 'conned' or guilty when you hear your Pastor ask for the offering?

___

Do you ever spend money on those less fortunate (outside of your family)?

____

Your sin

What is a habit, addiction, or selfish attitude that you refuse to give up to God?

____

Why are you finding it so hard to change or let go of it?

____

____

Do you *believe* that God can heal you or deliver you from this thing?

____

2. **If you do have fear about surrendering these areas to God, ask yourself "Why am I afraid"?**
   (examples may include "I'm not ready to give up the things I am doing", or, "I'm too busy to let God have any of my already limited time", or "I don't want to lose my friends/family/boyfriend, etc.", or "My money is my money - I earned it.....)

   ____

   ____

   ____

   ____

3. **Do you truly want to start living a more holy life? Why?**
   (examples may include "I'm miserable knowing what I should do and not doing it - I want to be more intimate with God", or "I'm tired of trying to live two different lives - I want to jump the fence and really commit myself to Him completely", or "I feel like a fraud– I'm really a different person when I'm home

than when I am out in public. I want to be the same person all of the time").

____

____

____

____

4. **What are some steps you might be able to take to accomplish the changes you want to make?**
(You might say "I will commit to reading the Bible for 20 minutes every day". Or, "I will commit to praying for a period of time every day so that I can purposefully meet with God", or "I will go out of my way to serve other people at least once a day").

____

____

____

____

5. **What is the worst that could happen if you started regularly submitting to God?**
(examples may include "I would be embarrassed to let others know that I am completely devoted to Jesus", or "I would have to change the people I hang out with", or "That would upset the superficial life I have with Jesus now - I'm fine just giving Him a part of my life".

____

____

____

____

PART II

THE FUNCTION OF DISCIPLESHIP

CHAPTER 7
SERVANTHOOD

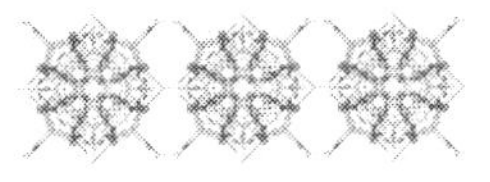

If I were to sum up "a Christian" in one word, it would be the word ***Servant***.

This may seem odd to you, because there are so many other wonderful words that might come to mind if you were to describe an authentic follower of Jesus Christ. Loving, joyful, generous, kind, respectful....these can (and should) be the characteristics of Christians. But *servanthood* is the basis for all of these traits.

As Christians, we have been bought with a precious and immeasurable price (1 Peter 1:18-20). Therefore, we are not only privileged, but obligated, to make sure that Jesus is continually elevated to His rightful place as our Master and Lord. This is the foundation of our faith. But unless we become humble servants, we will never mature as Christians, or experience the deep relationship God wants to have with us.

When we have the right attitude, we will desire to love the Lord and to surrender to Him. One beautiful byproduct of that love is service to others - *servanthood*. Consequently, the way we serve others will result in *being* loving, joyful, generous, kind, and respectful – the very qualities listed above!

Me, Myself, and Mine!

It's not difficult to see that the concept of serving has decreased drastically in our culture in the last few decades. This is one of the main reasons why we are in such disarray in our country. We have become "consumers" - far removed from being "servers". This mentality has also affected our churches today. Some consider it a great feat and sacrifice if they donate money to church, missions, or serve on a food line for the homeless once a month!

The root of this consumer mindset is "self". We have systematically taken God off the throne in our personal lives and in our country, and replaced Him with our own opinions, desires and indulgences. But in doing so, we have deteriorated from what was once a great nation to one of ridicule.

When we put ourselves above biblical standards and refuse to submit to God's will, we reap a dreadful harvest (Romans 1:18-32; Galatians 5:14-24; 2 Timothy 3:1-5). The apostle Paul uses the words "biting" and "devouring" in these passages. It reminds me of wild animals attacking one another, and I see this type of behavior regularly in our society!

"Self" always divides. Think about it. If everyone is "doing their own thing", then unity is impossible. When we have our eyes only on ourselves, we cannot look out to see others' needs. And if we are all going in our own direction, we have no common ground or goal (Proverbs 14:12). We lack the ability to help one another.

We may believe we are "getting what we want so we'll be happy" – in essence, loving ourselves. However, this behavior only leaves us fragmented, frustrated, disappointed, and alone. Actually, "loving" ourselves in this unhealthy way isn't really *love* at all (1 Corinthians 13:4-7). True love looks out, not in. And since **God** *is* Love, when we are removed from Him, we lose our capacity to genuinely love (1 John 4:8).

Now before you say "Well, I love my spouse, or my children, or my parents, so I don't need God's help to love anyone", we need to examine what *kind of love* we are speaking about. The type of love that is servant-based and outwardly-focused is called *agape (a-gop-eh)* in the original Greek language of the New Testament.

This is the pure love that comes from the heart of God the Father. It's the kind of love that sent His Son to the Cross. Jesus, in His love for us, allowed Himself to suffer an excruciating and forsaking death - so that many would be saved. God showed us a picture of real love by giving Himself away (Galatians 1:4; 1 John 3:16). It's a sacrificial love. *And it doesn't need a loving response in order to keep loving.*

In fact, the only reason we are able to love at all is because love has its origin in God (1 John 4:19). Humans are created in the image of God, so they derive their love from His character (Genesis 1:27). In essence, we all have the ability to reflect Him in certain areas of our lives, even when we aren't in relationship with Him. For example, our talents, our desire to help others, and appreciation for nature are all byproducts of being made in His likeness.

However, *agape* love is the direct outgrowth of the Holy Spirit living inside of us. This empowers us to think of others more highly than we think of ourselves (Philippians 2:3; Galatians 5:22). This kind of love, we read, is based in humility. And it naturally **serves** - even sacrificing for strangers and those we may find unlovable.

God First

We frequently like to think of ourselves as independent. In fact, we train our children to be self-sufficient from the beginning of their lives when they first learn to walk and talk. While it is good and healthy for humans to be able to take care of themselves, unfortunately, we have taken this mindset to the extreme.

This *self* attitude affects our minds, wills, emotions, and our conduct. When we feel we don't need God or others to help us, this all-encompassing self-reliance becomes unhealthy. Consequently, reliance and dependence on the Lord is seen as a "crutch".

What we focus our energy and affection towards - indeed, our heart and soul - is what we love and revere. It is essentially what we worship. Ironically, as independent as we may *think* we are, we all serve someone or something (Romans 6:16). Our actions reveal whom we truly serve; either God or ourselves.

Therefore, when our highest priorities are fixed on anyone or anything besides God, we are placing our adoration in the wrong place. That is exactly what brings so much dissatisfaction to our lives. We were *created* to love and serve God above all else!

We often fail to see that when we put ourselves, others, or "things" before God, we set ourselves up for failure. The truth is, God is the Only One who is truly worthy of absolute honor, respect and love. And the fruit we bear – the outcome of our decisions - is a witness to our heart's true intent. When we put God first, the outflow of our lives will be one of servanthood, because that is the heart of our Lord.

Now that certainly doesn't mean that taking care of ourselves is wrong! Some people "serve" God and others to the point of ignoring their own needs completely. They may even see this kind of service as a badge of honor. They get attention for all the work they are doing and play the martyr. Being a "doormat" is also an unhealthy extreme.

What Or Whom Do I Worship?

It is our choice as to what or to whom we devote our life. There is a reason why we call movie stars and famous sports people "idols"! We have all seen or heard about someone who seems to "have it all". We may envy their money, power, house, appearance, car, or status.

But if Christ is absent from their lives, they actually live a hollow existence deep inside. They often worship things and people, but in doing so, they reject God, who alone can bring deep joy and true satisfaction. In fact, the Hebrew word for "worship" is the same as the one used for "to be a slave of". Thus, whatever or whomever we worship, we are slaves to (2 Peter 2:19).

Now I have met people who say they are happy, but they don't have a relationship with Jesus. They feel their lives are complete without God. I believe you *can* have a relatively "good" life without the Lord....but.... these people are ignoring a big part of their human capacity - their spirit.

They will never experience the deep joy, hope, and purpose that God has ordained for them. They refuse to know and commune with the Savior. The most serious problem with this is that God doesn't say you will have eternal life if you are "happy" or "good". He makes it plain that without accepting Jesus Christ into your heart and life, you will not spend eternity with Him.

Then there are others who are completely absorbed with themselves. They constantly talk about *their* situation, accomplishments, and problems, but they rarely care about how others are doing. These people "worship" themselves. In doing so, they literally drain your energy, and you hardly ever feel better after visiting them! These two types of people have one thing in common: they do not serve others.

Jesus, The Servant

Jesus had a lot to say about being a server as He was training His disciples. We find a startling message in Matthew 20:25-28. The Greek word "slave" in this passage is "diakoneo", which is where we derive our English word "deacon". It is translated "to minister to"; "to be an attendant"; or "to menially wait upon (someone else) as a server".

To our human understanding, to be a slave of another is usually not an uplifting position. Yet our Lord is describing one of the most important ways to have an intimate relationship with Him, to advance His Kingdom purposes, and to obtain joy.

Jesus - God in the flesh, Co-Creator, King of all kings - incredibly said of Himself that "He came *to* serve, not to *be* served" (Matthew 12:18; Mark 10:45; Philippians 2:3-8). He came to sacrifice His blood so that we could become holy and enjoy a relationship with Him now and forevermore.

Jesus is even prophesied about in the Old Testament book of Isaiah. He is referred to as the "Suffering Servant" and the "Servant of the Lord" (Isaiah 42:1; 49:5-7; 52:13-15). What is astounding is that Jesus is referring to *Himself* in Luke 4:18-19. The Scripture He's talking about is from Isaiah 61:1-2, and that passage dates back to approximately 700 years before He was even born!

We balk at the idea of being a 'servant' in our society, because of the thoughts that are invoked by that word. Our culture often demeans those who are paid minimum wage or who serve others for a living. However, Jesus used this word purposefully, and He expected us to literally live out this *identity* in our lives, just as He Himself did (Isaiah 53).

There are many biblical meanings for being a slave or a servant. But one that categorizes our identity as our Lord's "slave" is beautifully captured in the Old Testament (Deuteronomy 15:12-17). We read in this account that if someone was in debt, he was to serve the person or family he was indebted to for 6 years. In the seventh year, he had to be set free.

However, there were times that the slave would have developed a deep love for the family over the years, and would decide to serve them willingly for the rest of his life. In this case, an awl (a piece of sharp flint, bone, stone or metal) would be driven through the slaves' ear, representing a lifetime of *desired* slavery.

This is an accurate picture of how our relationship with Jesus ought to be. He knows that if He has our whole mind, heart, will, soul, and strength, then He will be able to empower us to live a life far greater than the temporary, idolatry-filled lives we often choose when we are centered only on ourselves. Since Jesus Christ was sinless, He is the perfect example and leader for us to imitate when it comes to servanthood.

The apostle Paul often called himself a "bondslave" of Christ, and I just love that concept. The word for bondslave (many translations use 'servant' for the word 'bondslave') in the Greek is "doulos" which means "to be in subjection to", or "to be in bondage to". I absolutely want to be my Master's desirous, deeply-committed, always-willing, connected-to, and fully-surrendered bondslave! I want my Lord to be so pleased with me when I see Him face-to-face!

What Are You in Bondage To?

Of course, we also think of the word "bondage" in negative terms. But just think: if you were in "bondage" to Jesus the way you may be enslaved in any area of your life right now, wouldn't that be amazing? You would be **compelled** to do good! You **wouldn't be able to help yourself** when it came to being generous, kind, and compassionate! You **would have a hard time thinking of anything else**, but pleasing God! You would **put aside other interests and activities** just to give yourself to serving the Lord.

This is precisely what God meant when He commanded us to "Love the Lord God with all your heart, all your soul, all your mind, and all your strength" Deuteronomy 6:4-6 and Matthew 22:37

If we are not dedicated in mind, heart, body, and soul to the Lord, we will not have the desire to spend quality time with Him. We won't "feel" like reading the Bible, or give a portion of our finances to Him. We won't want to help someone in need.

But beware: if we are constantly putting our own wishes first, He will quietly slip out of our hearts and minds. This tragedy has become a reality for many well-meaning Christians. The truth is, it's harder to reconnect with the Lord after our backsliding than it is to ensure we maintain our intimacy with Him on a daily basis.

Our Lord also tells us that we must give our lives up, and turn from our selfish ways, IF we want to gain eternal life (Mark 8:34-38; John 12:25-26). This idea of surrender is not to say that our work for God rewards us with salvation, because only Christ's Blood Sacrifice does that. Salvation is a free gift - not earned.

But what the Scriptures are saying regarding eternal life, is that IF you are saved - "IF you are really Mine (Jesus') - then you will naturally give up your life for Me in service" (Romans 15:1-3; 2 Timothy 2:21). Love always serves.

There will be consistent evidence of godliness in the life of someone who lives for Jesus. Again, salvation is "free", but it cost God everything, and being a genuine disciple will surely cost us everything. Jesus wants our wholehearted commitment, not just half-hearted attempts (2 Chronicles 6:14)!

Why Do I Need to Serve?

Service is a part of our worship to God. An excellent question we can ask ourselves to determine what we are focusing our lives on is "What do I spend the most amount of my time, affection, thoughts, money, and energy doing?" This will enable us to shine the spotlight on our true motives and values.

Jesus often used nature as a way to convey spiritual truths. We can liken our service to a reservoir. If the water level gets too high, there is a relief valve – called the spillway - to let excess water out. So it is in our lives. Whatever we are "too full of" will automatically "spill out of us", whether it's good or rotten.

Additionally, if a lake has no inlet or outlet, it becomes stagnant and dries up. This is so true in our Christian faith. If we do not allow the Holy Spirit to fill our lives and then share what we have been given through service to others, we become dull, lifeless and malodorous!

And just as an apple tree cannot produce figs, a genuine Christian cannot live his or her life in self-absorption. The two are mutually exclusive, meaning only one part can be true. Either you are serving Jesus or you are serving yourself (Matthew 12:30).

If the Christian is living the majority of their life in a self-fulfilling, self indulgent, and self-exalted state, then he or she *must* get back to the Cross, repent, and turn once again to Christ's Lordship - to live in submission to His plan and will for their lives (Romans 12:1-2).

How Can I Become a Real Servant?

Ironically, it is only when we humble ourselves in a position of submission and surrender to God that we find *true* freedom and *pure* joy (Matthew 16:24-26; 2 Corinthians 3:17; Philippians 2:17). Just as it is with many principles in the Bible, it doesn't seem to make human sense. "To be first, you must be last. To give is more blessed than to receive. You must "die" in order to live. To gain, you must give". But God's ways and thoughts are so much higher than ours, and since He made us, He knows that if we live by His guidelines, we will find true fulfillment.

However, as we have read, humility needs to be present in order to be a good and faithful server. We have all met people who are in "server roles" but clearly do not serve with a giving and thoughtful attitude! A humble attitude is first realized in our relationship with God. If we don't have a spirit of humble-ness, we will lack the ability to give Him His rightful place of headship in our lives. We will fight to stay in control - and this position is contrary to the one we need as servants. We will never serve well if *being served* is our only motivation.

What Are Some Practical Ways to Serve God And Others?

1. The Bible says that God's people are a "Kingdom of Priests and a holy nation". This is true of both the Old Testament Israelites and the New Testament Christians (Exodus 19:5-6; 1 Peter 2:5-10). One of the main responsibilities of the priests was to lead people into a closer relationship with God.

   We should be listening and watching for opportunities to do this. Maybe we can buy someone a meal - and tell them about Jesus. Or help to mow someone's lawn - and tell them about Jesus! All of our efforts to help others should be laced with the Gospel; otherwise, it's just a humanitarian effort and there are plenty of organizations out there that fit that criteria.

2. As the above Scripture in Peter says, we can offer "spiritual sacrifices" to God. This means praising Him directly, as well as voicing our praise of Him out loud to others. I often say things in casual conversations, even with people I don't know, such as "Isn't it amazing the way God created this beautiful day?" Just putting God's name or His miraculous creativity out there can prompt others to think about Him.
3. The Scripture in Peter also says that we can show others the goodness of God. This can take the form of smiling at someone, encouraging them, rooting for those who are less able or fortunate, visiting someone who is shut in or in prison, or a myriad of other acts.

   Just remember, you are Christ's representative wherever you go. Doing things in His name (meaning with the intention of sharing Him) is your first priority. There is a chapter in this book called "Sharing Our Faith" and it will go into more detail about how to do this.
4. You can lead a Bible study with people who may not be knowledgeable about the Lord.
5. Pray about what God might have you do. Ask Him for opportunities to share Him with others, and for the exact people He might want you to impact. He'll answer your prayers if you're serious!

Are You Ready?

Jesus speaks frequently of our need to not only serve, but to be ready for His coming at all times. Part of our service to Him is to eagerly await and to be ready for His coming. His parable in Matthew 25:1-13 of the 10 Bridesmaids illustrates this truth. The 'oil' in this story represents the Holy Spirit, who is the One giving us the direction, power, and ability to be "ready".

Being ready means serving God by giving our lives away for His purposes. This story is meant to be a strong warning for the Christian. It is *in the very process* of serving Him that we are armed and ready for whatever comes our way. As I always say, "Whatever you are doing now is what you will do when your 'dreams' come true – or when tragedy strikes".

The subsequent story of the estate managers in Matthew 25:14-30 describes the same principle: BE READY! We cannot make decisions at the last moment when Jesus comes for His Bride in the Rapture. It's like a fruit tree that has been neglected. We can't just throw fertilizer and water on it after it has already shriveled, expecting it to come back to life. It takes time and effort to bring it back to proper health again.

It is *the steady feeding and watering over time* that makes the tree pleasing to look at and sit under, as well as making it healthy enough to bear fruit. May we, as Jesus' followers, be pleasing to the multitudes of parched souls we meet, and become the luscious fruit that will draw them closer to our beloved Savior!

CHAPTER 7
SERVANTHOOD
REFLECTION

1. **Would you describe yourself as a more of a selfish person or a server of others?**

   ____

   ____

2. **Would you say you focus more on the "things of this world" (i.e. clothes, money, school, job, electronics, etc...) than spiritual things?**

   ____

   ____

3. **Does the word "servant" or "server" make you feel uncomfortable? Why?**

   ____

   ____

   ____

4. **The Bible says that to become great in God's Kingdom, we must become a servant. Do you believe that's true?**

   ____

   ____

   Would you be willing to become more of a server than you may be now?

   ____

   ____

5. **What is one thing you can do to become more focused on God?**

____

____

6. **What is one thing you can do to become more focused on others' needs?**

____

____

CHAPTER 8
THE SPIRITUAL GIFTS

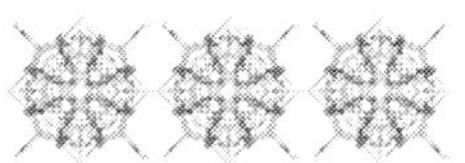

If you have been a Christian for any length of time, you have probably heard about "spiritual gifts". But you may not know what they really are. Or how to tell which gifts are yours. You may also be wondering how to use the gifts you have.

God gives each believer their own spiritual gifts when they receive salvation, when we became part of His Body, the Church (1 Corinthians 12: 5-11; Ephesians 4:11-13). These gifts should be used to glorify and bless God. They are also used particularly to serve other believers. But they are also useful to help those who are not followers of Jesus.

Service to our Master has many facets. As we *purposefully* serve God by serving others, we are proving our love for Him (John 14:15, 21, 23-24; John 15:10, 13-14, 17). Uniquely as believers, God designated every one of us a special ability to serve Him and others.

Unfortunately, some churches don't openly talk about, explore, or knowingly use the spiritual gifts. And other churches abuse the spiritual gifts by excluding or demeaning those who do not believe in or use certain gifts, such as speaking in tongues or healing.

The gifts are meant to help foster unity, not division. They are given to Christians to build each other up and to encourage each other. So if they are used to alienate, confuse, or degrade others, they are not being used properly.

And just because a church may be uncomfortable with tongues and healing does not mean they are not serving the Lord properly. Likewise, if the more "unusual" gifts *are* being used in a church, it doesn't mean they aren't Christians! But the gifts *should* be explored and used to some extent in every church.

Additionally, there are some people who believe the spiritual gifts are no longer in operation. They think they were used only in the early New Testament Church and don't apply to Christians today.

However, spiritual gifts are extremely important and essential tools that God gives to believers in serving the Body of Christ and to minister to the unsaved. This chapter will briefly outline what some of the gifts are and how we are to use them.

- Before we begin, you will need to fill out the Spiritual Gifts Inventory available at the end of this chapter. Please complete it and score your answers now, before you read the rest of this chapter.

Old Testament Spiritual Gifts?

Spiritual gifts are not specifically mentioned in the Old Testament like they are in the New Testament. God's people have always had spiritual gifts, to be sure, but they are only expressly outlined in the New Testament. The spiritual gifts are given to believers by the Spirit of God, who is Co-Creator, Eternal, and Pre-Existent.

That means He was not created. Just like Jesus and the Father, He existed *before* anything was created, and He is also fully God. The Holy Spirit was divinely active in human lives in the Old Testament for very specific purposes, events, individuals, and periods of time.

The Spirit of God came to live in *all* believers only after Jesus' ascension (John 14:15-17). Interestingly, Jesus says in this passage that the Holy Spirit is *with them* now (when Jesus was alive on earth before His ascension), but will be *in them* after He leaves.

I believe the reason the spiritual gifts were not active in every believer until the New Testament is because the Holy Spirit did not yet live inside of people, and His gifts were not poured out on Christ's followers until the day of Pentecost (Acts 2:32-33; 1 Corinthians 6:19-20).

Additionally, the Bible says that the spiritual gifts are for the **Church** - to edify it, sustain it, build it up, and bring it to maturity; and the Church did not exist until Jesus left the earth (John 16:7). In fact, the first time the word "church" is even mentioned in the entire Bible is in Matthew 16:18!

This is not to say that God's people in the Old Testament were not "moved" or empowered by the Spirit, because the Bible clearly states that **all** of Scripture was inspired by Him (2 Timothy 3:16-17; 2 Peter 1:20-21). Every one of the biblical writers were led by the Spirit. And of course, many other people were "moved" by the Spirit in the Old Testament (Exodus 35:31; 2 Chronicles 24:20, to name a couple of instances). Additionally, God gifted them all with special abilities.

Meaning of the Word "Gift"

It is interesting to find that the word "gifts" in relation to spiritual gifts is a different word in the Greek than the common meaning of the word "gift" as it relates to a present. It is the word "charisma", which we all understand in English to mean "having the gift of drawing people; having charm, appeal, or magnetism". But in the original Greek, it means "a divine gratuity" or "a spiritual endowment". Spiritual gifts are, indeed, divinely endowed, purpose-laden attributes given to the genuine Christian.

This word charisma is also translated as "deliverance from danger or passion", which is easily seen as a positive byproduct in our lives when we are living in the Spirit and using our spiritual gifts! Satan is NOT happy when we are operating in the power of the Holy Spirit and doing God's Kingdom work! There is often a protective element when we are operating in our gifts.

Even though the spiritual gifts are purposed for the Church, they innately spill over into our ministry with the lost. For example, the gift of generosity or hospitality or teaching can definitely be helpful in drawing seekers of God into the Body of Christ.

A spiritual gift is the primary method by which the Holy Spirit ministers *through* the believer. It is a supernatural capacity for service to God - and He gives us tremendous desire to perform the duties of that gift. The gifts are a source of joy in the Christian life! They are a divine calling with a divine responsibility, because what God has gifted you to do, He has called you to do. And what He has called you to do, He has gifted you to do (Hebrews13:20-21).

Spiritual Gifts Versus Talent

Spiritual gifts differ from our "talents". Talents are also God-given, because all humans are made in the image of God, whether they are atheists or true believers. You don't need to believe in God to have 'talent'. But talents relate more to our natural bent, what we're good at doing as "humans".

We may even find that our talents and spiritual gifts are similar. For example, we may have talent in being a support to others even before we're saved. After salvation, the Spirit may give us the gift of "Encourager" (similar to supporting others).

The difference is that our spiritual gift is an extra measure of power in this area, and it is given specifically so that the Church may grow in fullness and maturity (Ephesians 4:11-13). But remember that the Church is built up not only for its own edification, but in order to spill out into the world, becoming a beacon of light and hope for the lost.

Additionally, Spiritual Gifts are *Spirit led, not of human power.* Even if your church doesn't necessarily "operate" in the gifts (such as teaching about them and delegating responsibilities in the church according to the gifts), you are responsible to the Lord to use the gifts He has given you. Be aware that spiritual gifts *always* involve people, and they always involve actions to help others.

The best way to prove that your gift(s) are genuine is 1. You enjoy using your gift; it isn't a burden, and 2. Others in the Body confirm that as you use your gift, their lives are enriched. In essence, confirmation of your gifts will come from the church. The end result of our gifts should be an obvious blessing to others.

Just a word of caution: the gifts can certainly be misused and distorted, mainly because of our sin nature. For example, with the "extraverted" gifts (Pastor, Teacher, Leadership, Evangelist), pride and self-sufficiency can become a real obstacle. When people are frequently praised for their gift, it can cause them to take the credit that God alone deserves.

With the potentially "introverted" gifts (Service, Kindness, Giver), one can become self-sacrificing in an unhealthy way, in an attempt to feel worthy or to be included. Being a martyr for "self" is never attractive.

These people may also have the tendency of being taken advantage of, because they love to serve.

Of course, this is not to say that only people with these particular gifts will experience these problems. But if these are your gifts, just be aware of the potential pitfalls. This is why it is so important to continue to personally grow in Christ, so that when our gifts are used, they are truly used for others, they are a healthy benefit to us, and they glorify God.

Learning what our gifts are, as well as how to use them, is fun! However, like any new undertaking, they must be experimented with, and frequently used, in order for us to become proficient in them. As you use your gift(s), it will guide your service for the Lord in a more productive and pleasing way.

Again, the purpose of the gifts is *always* other-focused, and Christ needs to be the primary motivator for using them. Above all, they are for **God's** glory, not to meet our own agendas.

So, What Are The Gifts?

There are several passages of Scripture which list the gifts. Scholars differ as to the number of gifts that are listed in the Bible, but we will deal with a few of the specific ones mentioned in the following Scriptures. We have already read Ephesians 4:11-13.

Let's also read Romans 12:3-8; 1 Corinthians, Chapters 12 and 14;and 1 Peter 4:7-11

I would like to mention that there are times when even if you don't have a particular gift, you are still responsible to walk in that arena. For example, maybe you haven't been given the *gift* of "Generous Giver", but that does not mean that you *shouldn't be* a generous giver. Similarly, you may not have the *gift* of being a Server, but it doesn't mean you are not to serve others regularly.

Conversely, there are some gifts that *are* only to be used by the ones who are given their particular gift, such as teacher, leader, and pastor. When people try to use those types of gifts when God has not given them, it can be disastrous.

We've all been "led" by those who *think* they're good bosses or leaders or pastors (but they are not); or we've been taught by those who *think* they teach well (but they don't).... We will know if these folks are truly gifted or not by the results of their efforts.

<u>Specific Gifts</u>

This section is simply an overview of the gifts. There are many good books and websites available to study them indepth. I haven't listed them all, but for the purpose of discussion, I have expanded on some of them here:

Prophecy: This *can* be the gift of being able to foresee the future, and it was prevalent among the Old Testament prophets. Much of the future prophecy we read about then was recorded because the entirety of Scriptures had not been written yet.

It was also used to validate God's message to the people. Of course, only God knows what will happen in the future. So He would tell the prophets what was going to happen, and when the event came to pass, the people's faith was strengthened and unbelieving people came to the Lord. I believe prophets who predict the future still exist, though they are rare (Jeremiah 28:9).

However, the more common, and certainly, the most beneficial, meaning of prophecy is "the ability to explain the Scriptures in a way that the hearer can understand them". Those with this gift also strengthen, encourage, and comfort other believers with their message (or teaching) (1 Corinthians 14:3).

Service: This gift is also called the "Gift of Helps". It is an unusual passion to serve others, often at great sacrifice to themselves. They like "being behind the scenes" and don't want attention called to themselves. Again, we are all responsible to serve one another, but this gifted person does so with the most extraordinary pleasure and final results!

Teacher: This gift is self-explanatory. The way to know if it is effective, though, is to monitor growth in those you are teaching. If this is a true gift, people should not only be interested when you teach, but they should be motivated to action by your instruction.

Encourager: This gift is also called "The Gift of Exhortation". This often means "to urge, or to move others into action". It comes from the

Greek word "paracletos" which means 'to call to one's side' or 'to come alongside'. It is a picture of someone walking beside you, helping to motivate you, keeping you on track, and assisting you if you falter. In fact, the Holy Spirit is called "The Paraclete", as He is our Helper, Comforter, and Advocate (John 14:16; 15:26).

Leadership: This may seem like an obvious title, but it needs some explanation. First of all, true leaders in the church are called by the Lord; they are not self-appointed (1 Corinthians 1:1). A gifted leader is one who leads by example, and who is willing to be a servant to those whom he/she leads (Matthew 20:25-28). This does not mean being a "doormat". These types of leaders have very strong character and should be respected. But their motive will be one of a willing server. Our Lord was the perfect example of this Servant-Leader attitude.

If you encounter a "leader" who has not actually been given this gift, he/she will be arrogant and proud, difficult to approach, harsh and critical, and believe it's "their way or the highway". They will lack the ability to accept criticism or instruction.

Kindness: We are all called to be kind (Galatians 5:22; Ephesians 4:30-32). The word used here is *chrestos*, which means "fit for use"! We are most useful to God when we are kind; somewhat like the old saying 'It's easier to attract with honey than with vinegar'!

It also means "to have mercy". *Mercy* means not giving people what they deserve, which is how God abundantly treats us. Therefore, we are to use it in abundance with others. Interestingly, in the Hebrew language, the word kindness is often used to describe the **value** of gemstones.

Pastor: The Greek word "poimen" means pastor. Although the word "poimen" is translated as 'pastor' infrequently in the Bible, it is translated as "shepherd" in most places. Therefore, we are actually discussing the GIFT of shepherding, not the POSITION of pastor. Though a good pastor must have the gift of shepherding, those who have the gift of shepherding are not necessarily a pastor. Those who naturally draw groups of people to themselves who are looking for spiritual advice and mentoring fit this gift.

Generous Giver: On first impression, "giving" usually brings *money* to mind. But those with the gift of giving have an unusual ability to see others' needs, and to fill them. This can pertain to physical, mental, emotional, spiritual, and financial needs. It is an extra measure of delight that this believer receives in attending to people so they can become whole.

Giver of wise advice: This applies to biblical wisdom. The word 'wisdom' comes from the Greek word "sophia". It is the ability not only to live in godliness, but to be able to show and teach others how to apply scriptural truths to their lives in a manner that makes the most sense for that hearer. Wisdom is *living out* that which you have learned (knowledge) from the Bible and the Spirit of God.

Special Knowledge: This is the God-given ability to understand the deep meaning of the Bible. It is intended for this individual to share biblical knowledge with others. It is also a form of discernment, which is being able to "see" into spiritual matters without really having any proof.

Faith: We all have faith, otherwise we wouldn't be Christians! But some people are given an extraordinary measure of faith, and this gift is intended to stimulate other believers in *their* potential to believe that God is who He says He is and that He rewards those who seek Him (Hebrews 11:6). This person has the ability to increase the faith of others.

Healer: It seems as if there is less "physical" healing happening today, especially in the more industrialized nations. I believe part of this is because healing is so sensationalistic, and people have a great tendency to worship the person performing the healing, rather than the Great Physician Himself, Jesus Christ.

I also think healing is more prevalent in third world countries because many people have never heard the Gospel, and miracles prove God's power and existence. The people in these cultures also have overwhelming faith that has not been tainted by repeatedly rejecting God's message.

Studies have been done which have found that people with higher education and income not only *believe* less in healing, but *experience* it less frequently (Barna Study, *Most Americans Believe in Supernatural Healing* – 2016).

Performing Miracles: God is a miraculous God! He does not change, so I know He continues to perform miracles around the world on a daily basis. But just like healing, true miracles (which are events that cannot be explained by human effort or achievement) seem to happen more often amongst those who actually believe they exist. Also, miracles are often manifested as unusual timing and events.

It also seems that Christians who live in countries where they are greatly persecuted for their faith witness more miracles (including physical healings) than the American Church. For example, it is well known that the underground church in Iran is the fastest growing church in the world right now, and much of it is because Jesus is "visiting" people in visions and dreams.

Discernment: Basic discernment is the ability to tell good from evil, and sense when things are "amiss", such as when danger is present without any reasonable signs. Since we have the Holy Spirit living in us, discernment is available in some measure to all believers. And the more we get to know God and His Word, the more discernment we will develop (Hebrews 5:11-14). Another word for "recognize" in the NLT Bible is "discern".

However, God does give some the "gift" of discernment (1 Corinthians 12:10). As mentioned previously, this is an extra measure of discernment which is the unusual ability to see deeply into *spiritual* situations that are otherwise not apparent. Christians with this gift make very good counselors.

Tongues and Interpretation of Tongues: This gift is one of the most abused and misunderstood gifts of all. The gift of tongues was used in the Book of Acts to validate the spiritual authority of the Apostles (1 Corinthians 14:22). This tongue-speaking was not simply "utterances", as it is often seen today. It was literally speaking in other languages so that the people groups present were able to understand their own language (Acts 2:4). That was a real miracle and convinced people that God's power was present in His followers!

Today, the gift of tongues is (or should be) used mainly between a believer and the Lord (1 Corinthians 14:2). It is meant to be a vehicle of deeper communication in our relationship with Him. Not everyone has the gift of tongues (1 Corinthians 12:30). However, some churches that overly focus on this gift may exclude those who do not speak in tongues; sometimes going as far as to say that "non-tongue" speaking people are not Christians! This is definitely not biblical.

There are also situations where someone in a congregation will speak in tongues, but there are 2 criteria to determine if it's from the Lord: First, there needs to be an interpreter present - someone who has a God-given ability to understand and speak out to the church what was said (1 Corinthians 14:5, 13, and 26). Secondly, it needs to be done in an orderly fashion (1 Corinthians 14:29).

I don't agree with a church that allows people to roam the building speaking loud, unintelligible utterances. This does not create a spirit of unity or love, and often makes outsiders feel unwelcome and very uncomfortable – both of which are detrimental!

I have been in services like this on several occasions, and the Spirit seemed nowhere to be found. I believe that when a service or gathering in Christ's Name is so disruptive that you can't focus on the Lord, there is a problem.

I understand there will be those who disagree with my assessment. We must treat each other lovingly and respectfully, regardless of our differences. I simply am stating what I feel I have learned from Scripture and have seen in person.

And of course, this is not to say it is not healthy or good to speak in tongues. It just needs to be done in a godly way to bring the most benefit to those with the gift (and the hearers, if fitting), and glory to God.

Helper: This is the gift of someone who is willing to support others without receiving much attention, or possibly even gratitude for their gift. They may even prefer to work behind the scenes, and they experience great joy when others receive applause or credit. They are a unique and special group of people.

Evangelist: This is the person who is able to talk to anyone (and I mean ANYONE ☺) about Jesus. But not only are they able to talk about the Lord, they have the gift of explaining spiritual principles so that others can understand them clearly. They also enable others to desire the gift a relationship with Jesus that may lead to salvation.

It truly is a gift to be able to present the Gospel without being abrasive, while at the same time, being bold enough to share the truth with others. Additionally, ALL Christians are called to share their faith, in some measure, with those in their sphere of influence. The excuse "Well, I'm not an evangelist" doesn't excuse a Christ-follower from witnessing!

Summary

So remember, God has already given us our gifts when we received salvation. We have everything we need to serve Him (1 Corinthians 1:4-9). Our job is to find out what our gifts are through exploration and testing. Then we are to use our gifts with all the strength and energy that God supplies. As already mentioned, we know when we are operating in our genuine gifts when we love using them, people are positively impacted, AND they bring glory to the Lord.

I pray that through this study, you have gained a deeper understanding of what it is to be able to use the wonderful gifts that God has given you. Hopefully, you have become more aware of your gifts, and are excited to begin finding out where you truly fit into the Body of Christ as God has endowed you!

CHAPTER 8
THE SPIRITUAL GIFTS
REFLECTION

1. **Why did God give the Church Spiritual Gifts?**

2. **What is your top gift according to the Spiritual Gifts Inventory? If you have more than one gift according to the highest number, list that as well.**

3. **Knowing your gift, are you willing to discover how to use it?**

4. **What steps might you take in order to start using your gift?**

Please note that with this Spiritual Gifts Inventory, you need to ask Jesus into your heart and life, and have the Holy Spirit living within you in order for this questionnaire to have any meaning. This is because people who are not Christians have not been given Spiritual Gifts.

SPIRITUAL GIFTS SURVEY

DIRECTIONS

This is not a test, so there are no wrong answers. The ***Spiritual Gifts Survey*** consists of 80 statements. Some items reflect concrete actions; other items are descriptive traits; and still others are statements of belief.

- Select the one response you feel best characterizes yourself and place that number in the blank provided. Record your answer in the blank beside each item.
- Do not spend too much time on any one item. Remember, it is not a test. Usually your immediate response is best.
- Please give an answer for each item. Do not skip any items.
- Do not ask others how they are answering or how they think you should answer.
- Work at your own pace.

Your response choices are:

5—Highly characteristic of me/definitely true for me
4—Most of the time this would describe me/be true for me
3—Frequently characteristic of me/true for me–about 50 percent of the time
2—Occasionally characteristic of me/true for me–about 25 percent of the time
1—Not at all characteristic of me/definitely untrue for me

___ 1. I have the ability to organize ideas, resources, time, and people effectively.
___ 2. I am willing to study and prepare for the task of teaching.
___ 3. I am able to relate the truths of God to specific situations.

___ 4. I have a God-given ability to help others grow in their faith.

___ 5. I possess a special ability to communicate the truth of salvation.

___ 6. I have the ability to make critical decisions when necessary.

___ 7. I am sensitive to the hurts of people.

___ 8. I experience joy in meeting needs through sharing possessions.

___ 9. I enjoy studying.

___ 10. I have delivered God's message of warning and judgment.

___ 11. I am able to sense the true motivation of persons and movements.

___ 12. I have a special ability to trust God in difficult situations.

___ 13. I have a strong desire to contribute to the establishment of new churches.

___ 14. I take action to meet physical and practical needs rather than merely talking about or planning to help.

___ 15. I enjoy entertaining guests in my home.

___ 16. I can adapt my guidance to fit the maturity of those working with me.

___ 17. I can delegate and assign meaningful work.

___ 18. I have an ability and desire to teach.

___ 19. I am usually able to analyze a situation correctly.

___ 20. I have a natural tendency to encourage others.

___ 21. I am willing to take the initiative in helping other Christians grow in their faith.

___ 22. I have an acute awareness of the emotions of other people, such as loneliness, pain, fear, and anger.

___ 23. I am a cheerful giver.

___ 24. I spend time digging into facts.

___ 25. I feel that I have a message from God to deliver to others.

___ 26. I can recognize when a person is genuine/honest.

___ 27. I am a person of vision (a clear mental portrait of a preferable future given by God). I am able to communicate vision in such a way that others commit to making the vision a reality.

___ 28. I am willing to yield to God's will rather than question and waver.

___ 29. I would like to be more active in getting the gospel to people in other lands.
___ 30. It makes me happy to do things for people in need.
___ 31. I am successful in getting a group to do its work joyfully.
___ 32. I am able to make strangers feel at ease.
___ 33. I have the ability to plan learning approaches.
___ 34. I can identify those who need encouragement.
___ 35. I have trained Christians to be more obedient disciples of Christ.
___ 36. I am willing to do whatever it takes to see others come to Christ.
___ 37. I am attracted to people who are hurting.
___ 38. I am a generous giver.
___ 39. I am able to discover new truths.
___ 40. I have spiritual insights from Scripture concerning issues and people that compel me to speak out.
___ 41. I can sense when a person is acting in accord with God's will.
___ 42. I can trust in God even when things look dark.
___ 43. I can determine where God wants a group to go and help it get there.
___ 44. I have a strong desire to take the gospel to places where it has never been heard.
___ 45. I enjoy reaching out to new people in my church and community.
___ 46. I am sensitive to the needs of people.
___ 47. I have been able to make effective and efficient plans for accomplishing the goals of a group.
___ 48. I often am consulted when fellow Christians are struggling to make difficult decisions.
___ 49. I think about how I can comfort and encourage others in my congregation.
___ 50. I am able to give spiritual direction to others.
___ 51. I am able to present the gospel to lost persons in such a way that they accept the Lord and His salvation.
___ 52. I possess an unusual capacity to understand the feelings of those in distress.

___ 53. I have a strong sense of stewardship based on the recognition that God owns all things.

___ 54. I have delivered to other persons messages that have come directly from God.

___ 55. I can sense when a person is acting under God's leadership.

___ 56. I try to be in God's will continually and be available for His use.

___ 57. I feel that I should take the gospel to people who have different beliefs from me.

___ 58. I have an acute awareness of the physical needs of others.

___ 59. I am skilled in setting forth positive and precise steps of action.

___ 60. I like to meet visitors at church and make them feel welcome.

___ 61. I explain Scripture in such a way that others understand it.

___ 62. I can usually see spiritual solutions to problems.

___ 63. I welcome opportunities to help people who need comfort, consolation, encouragement, and counseling.

___ 64. I feel at ease in sharing Christ with nonbelievers.

___ 65. I can influence others to perform to their highest God-given potential.

___ 66. I recognize the signs of stress and distress in others.

___ 67. I desire to give generously and unpretentiously to worthwhile projects and ministries.

___ 68. I can organize facts into meaningful relationships.

___ 69. God gives me messages to deliver to His people.

___ 70. I am able to sense whether people are being honest when they tell of their religious experiences.

___ 71. I enjoy presenting the gospel to persons of other cultures and backgrounds.

___ 72. I enjoy doing little things that help people.

___ 73. I can give a clear, uncomplicated presentation.

___ 74. I have been able to apply biblical truth to the specific needs of my church.

___ 75. God has used me to encourage others to live Christlike lives.

___ 76. I have sensed the need to help other people become more effective in their ministries.

___ 77. I like to talk about Jesus to those who do not know Him.

___ 78. I have the ability to make strangers feel comfortable in my home.

___ 79. I have a wide range of study resources and know how to secure information.

___ 80. I feel assured that a situation will change for the glory of God even when the situation seems impossible.

SCORING

Follow these directions to figure your score for each spiritual gift.

1. Place in each box your numerical response (1-5) to the item number which is indicated below the box.
2. For each gift, add the numbers in the boxes and put the total in the TOTAL box.
3. The responses with the highest number(s) are your strongest gifts

LEADERSHIP

Item 6 ____Item 16 ____ Item 27 ____ Item 43 ____ Item 65 ____
TOTAL ____

ADMINISTRATION

Item 1 ____ Item 17 ____ Item 31 ____ Item 47 ____ Item 59 ____
TOTAL ____

TEACHING

Item 2 ____ Item 18 ____ Item 33 ____ Item 61 ____ Item 73 ____
TOTAL ____

KNOWLEDGE

Item 9 ____ Item 24 ____ Item 39 ____ Item 68 ____ Item 79 ____
TOTAL ____

WISDOM
Item 3 ____ Item 19 ____ Item 48 ____ Item 62 ____ Item 74 ____
TOTAL _____

PROPHECY
Item 10 ____ Item 25 ____ Item 40 ____ Item 54 ____ Item 69 ____
TOTAL ____

DISCERNMENT
Item 11 ____ Item 26 ____ Item 41 ____ Item 55 ____ Item 70 ____
TOTAL ____

EXHORTATION
Item 20 ____ Item 34 ____ Item 49 ____ Item 63 ____ Item 75 ____
TOTAL ____

SHEPHERDING
Item 4 ____ Item 21 ____ Item 35 ____ Item 50 ____ Item 76 ____
TOTAL _____

FAITH
Item 12 ____ Item 28 ____ Item 42 ____ Item 56 ____ Item 80 ____
TOTAL ____

EVANGELISM
Item 5 ____ Item 36 ____ Item 51 ____ Item 64 ____ Item 77 ____
TOTAL _____

APOSTLESHIP
Item 13 ____ Item 29 ____ Item 44 ____ Item 57 ____ Item 71 ____
TOTAL ____

SERVICE/HELPS
Item 14 ____ Item 30 ____ Item 46 ____ Item 58 ____ Item 72 ____
TOTAL ____

MERCY
Item 7 ____ Item 22 ____ Item 37 ____ Item 52 ____ Item 66 ____
TOTAL ____

GIVING
Item 8 ____ Item 23 ____ Item 38 ____ Item 53 ____ Item 67 ____
TOTAL ____

HOSPITALITY
Item 15 ____ Item 32 ____ Item 45 ____ Item 60 ____ Item 78 ____
TOTAL ____

CHAPTER 9

SHARING OUR FAITH

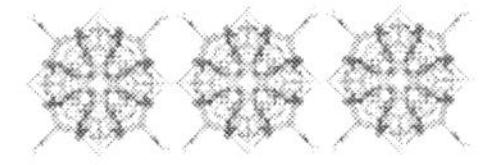

Word of-mouth has been proven to be one of the most effective ways to influence other people than any other means in history. Once someone has tried a great product or has gone to an awesome event, they naturally tell others about it. Experiencing something carries a lot more weight with the person you are trying to persuade than if you had just read it in a book or magazine.

What we think upon, what we are absorbed with, and what we are *passionate* about is what we tend to share with others. Whether we are consumed with our sports team, our children, our pets, cars, our job, money, etc., it will be our focal point and the basis of our conversation.

Similarly, if we are zealous for God, our lives will center around His thoughts and plans. Matthew 12:34c says it well: *"For whatever is in your heart determines what you say".*

Witnessing

We often hear the word "witness" and think of people banging on our door at very inconvenient times, so they can quote a bunch of Scriptures and tell us what a horrible job we're doing of running our lives. But Jesus has a much different approach. He wants us to live our lives so that when we open our mouths to share our faith, people will not see huge inconsistencies (Colossians 4:5-6).

The English word for witness means "to see, to observe, to view, or to perceive". It is used for 1. What we *see*, as well as 2. Verbalizing *what we have seen.* If you think about it, what good is a "witness" if they don't SPEAK?

Another interesting point is that the Greek translation for *witness* in the New Testament is *martus (mar-toos)*, which is where we derive our English word "martyr". It's quite possible the Lord knew we would be rebuffed for our faith ☺. While none of us likes to be rejected or outcast, the bottom line is that if we are genuine Christians, we need to be obedient to God, not afraid of man.

Sharing our faith because we love Jesus is one of the *most important* things we can possibly do in our Christian walk. Imparting our faith to others is an act of worship. We demonstrate our love for God by telling people how beautiful He is, and how He has changed our lives so incredibly. It is also a mandate from the Lord that we share Him with others. We are His representatives on this earth (2 Corinthians 5:18-21; Galatians 1:15-16a).

Mark 8:35 explains that we essentially gain *real* life when we give ourselves away for His sake and for the sake of *the Good News* - the Gospel. A huge part of serving God is sharing Jesus with others. One of the ways we do this is by living a life of holiness, and exhibiting winsome qualities so that people are attracted to *Jesus in us*, so they will want Him for themselves!

So many of us are missing out on the joy and excitement that comes from telling others about our Lord! It has the potential to shake your foundation and knock you out of your comfort zone - if you will only allow it!

The Lord *expects* us to tell others about what *we have seen and experienced in Him.* Scriptures are replete in the Old Testament as well as the New, to "tell others about God" (Psalm 71:7-8, 14-16; 96:1-10). A large part of our service to the Lord is **verbalizing** to others as to why we have faith in Him, and being available to minister to others in Jesus' Name whenever the Holy Spirit leads (I Peter 3:15).

We have <u>a debt of love to give back</u> to our Savior. And *HE is the One who lets us know that sharing Him with others is one of the ways He wants us to love Him and serve Him* (John 4:34-38). As difficult as sharing your faith may be for you, it is essential for your growth, and for the growth of God's Kingdom!

Jesus tells us that the harvest is ripe (Matthew 9:35-38). That means there are many people who are ready to receive the gospel message - and begin a new life in Christ. But someone has to tell them (Romans 10:14-17)! We have gotten into the mentality that "someone else will do it" or "I'm not equipped or ready to share my faith". We tell ourselves "They will know I'm a Christian by the way I act" and "I don't want to push my beliefs on others". If we're honest, though, we will admit that we are using this as an excuse because really don't *want* to share our faith.

When we are filled with the Holy Spirit at salvation, we receive power. But this isn't just any old power - it's the same power that raised Jesus from the dead (Ephesians 1:19-20)! Wow! And one of the main reasons we receive this power is *so that* we **can and will** be witnesses to the lost (Acts 1:8; Ephesians 3:7). God isn't just giving us a suggestion or hinting at a possibility here. He is *commanding* us to share our faith. The truth is that we *will* witness for Him if we love Him and have the Holy Spirit working in us.

Just think about the sports "fanatic". We think it's perfectly normal for him to rant and rave about his team. We see nothing wrong with him dressing up in crazy costumes, spending wads of money, driving across country for a big game, and jumping up and down screaming when his team is winning (or losing!) But if a Christian gets excited about their faith or they raise their hands in church, they're considered really weird and "out there". Go figure.

Fear

Let's face it - fear is probably the main reason we don't tell others about Jesus. We are embarrassed, thinking that people will reject our message, which, in essence, we feel, is a rejection of *us.* But Jesus makes it clear that if we reject Him in front of others, He will reject us before His Father and the angels (Matthew 10:33; Mark 8:38)! Maybe we're afraid we will lose friends, be excluded, or look weird. But we need to ask ourselves "Is my fear of man stronger than my love for the Lord?"

Self-centeredness is the root of our fear. Either we want to preserve our "persona", our "reputation"; or we want to protect ourselves from attack. Think about it, though. If we have built a persona or reputation that isn't centered on Jesus, then it is a "false self".

We are only our authentic "selves" when we are in Christ, because that's how He created us. Sin is what robs us of this reality. If we are trying to protect ourselves, we are putting ourselves on the throne, because God Himself is our Protector. If preserving or protecting ourselves is the basis for not sharing the Gospel with others, then we need to ask God for power to overcome this fear (Philippians 1:20).

On the other hand, if we are "other centered" and we truly care about others, we will remember that they are *eternally lost* if they don't receive salvation. We will be able to see past their false bravado, and see that without Jesus, they are unable to change and become Christ-like. Our spiritual eyes will be opened and we'll recognize that so many people are in emotional, mental, and relational pain, as well as deep bondage. They need prayer, deliverance, and a loving Savior. They need Jesus.

P.C.

Another huge problem is that "Political Correctness" has infiltrated not only our culture, but the Church, as well. Our mouths are sealed shut from sharing truth because, heaven forbid, we would offend someone! But I never see my Lord stepping on eggshells when He shares His Truth with His disciples, or sinners, or backslidden believers, so neither will I.

Now this doesn't mean we just go around beating people over the head with the Bible and tearing them down because of their sinful lifestyles. It does mean that we must "Speak the truth IN LOVE" (Ephesians 4:15). Our motive has to be loving and pure, because we care that they either come to know God or are restored back to God. We must be graceful and kind when we share.

There is an art to refraining from speaking when we have nothing nice to say! But being politically correct really means that we are lying to ourselves and others, and flattery is usually the culprit. Flattery is being untruthful in order to gain approval or acceptance. All of this is false behavior, and we will lose our moral compass if we continue to act towards others in this way (John 7:16-18).

God is clear in His Word that it is every Christian's responsibility - and **privilege** - to speak the Gospel message into others' lives. While it is true that we need to be *living* examples of holiness, faithfulness, and truthfulness, the Bible is explicit in instructing us to *verbalize* our faith. While none of us is perfect or sinless, the Lord uses *us* to offer salvation to those who are going to hell without Him.

We read the meaning of the Gospel in a nutshell in Acts 22:14-16. I will take the liberty of reversing the order of this Scripture to clarify my point:

Verse 16:
Call on the Name of the Lord
Have your sins washed away
"Get up" and be baptized

Verse 15:
Be His witness, conveying what you have seen and heard

Verse 14:
God has chosen us to know His will, which is to:
come to repentance
receive salvation
be baptized,
witness our faith
and to know, see, and hear from Jesus, the Righteous One

The Bible also says that we are to *make disciples*, which means we need to enter into relationship with others so we can lead them to salvation, and subsequently teach them what the Christian faith is all about (Matthew 28: 18-20). While most people won't get the opportunity to disciple the masses, we can certainly share with those in our sphere of influence.

One disciple is all it takes - if they are loved and taught properly, then they can go out and replicate what they have learned, and more people will be brought into the Kingdom of God. Just think: What will you say to Jesus on that day if you haven't brought *one person* with you?

What If I Get Rejected?

I always think of Jesus when I consider experiencing rejection for sharing my faith. He was scorned, spit upon, hated, run out of town, and eventually crucified, *just* for sharing that He was the Way to salvation and eternal life. But He was willing to go through all of this because He loved people! He saw past the anger and the hatred, and He looked deeply into their hearts. This is what gave Him such boldness.

He was so confident because He had only ONE purpose in mind: obedience to His Father. Jesus was on a mission, and nothing was going to stop Him from carrying out God's commands. The Father sent Jesus **to die for us**! Just think - what if He had shrunk back from the Cross? What if He had kept His mouth shut? We would have had no remedy to allow us a restored relationship with God. And we offer the exact same message to the lost - a *real solution* for true peace, love, and healing.

If we get rejected, it's really not the worst thing in the world!

Let's think about some of the "worst" things we fear that might happen if we begin to share Jesus with others:

- *Maybe you will lose a "friend"*. But were they really your friend in the first place, if they reject your choice to follow Christ? There are times in our Christian walk that we may need to distance ourselves from our friends or relatives, because of their open rejection of Christ (1 Corinthians 15:33; James 4:4). And truthfully, this may even relate to friends who "say" they are Christians, but do not live at all like Jesus (1 Corinthians 5:11)!

  I continue to pray for reconciliation for those relationships from which I must depart , but I know I need to guard and protect my relationship with Christ above all else (Proverbs 4:23). Now this doesn't mean we keep away from everyone who isn't a Christian... otherwise, we wouldn't be able to share with the unsaved. But it pertains to our close relationships – those with whom we spend the most time and intimacy.

- *Maybe you will get a "reputation".* Guess what? I have one, and I'm proud of it! Almost everyone I come in contact with discovers at some point that I'm in love with Jesus. What's interesting about this is that I'm often the one they turn to when they are in trouble, or have problems, or are in despair. They know I will pray for them, tell them the truth, and show them the Savior. It's wonderful to be counted as faithful to God!
- *Maybe you will be separated from your loved one.* I have experienced this in my own life. Jesus warned us that this may very well happen if we are genuinely devoted to Him (Matthew 10:34-39). Our values may be so offensive to those who are close to us, they may decide they don't want to hear about God anymore. They may feel very uncomfortable around us and convicted by our Christian lifestyle. If our walk with God is authentic, it WILL offend people, because Jesus **is** the "Rock of Offense" (1 Peter 2:7-8).
- *Maybe you will even be persecuted.* America is in deep trouble right now. There are more Christians in the world who are being rejected, beaten, imprisoned, and killed for their steadfast commitment to Christ than at any other time in history.
- We need to resolve in our hearts and minds that we love Jesus more than anything else, because wherever you live, you may be the next to experience persecution. In essence, *this* is where the rubber meets the road - being embarrassed isn't really a legitimate reason *not* to share our faith with others.

  However, let me encourage you by saying that every time I have obeyed God over people in my life, no matter how painful or uncomfortable it was, I have truly been able to count it as joy. Why? Because I know that if I weren't living a powerful life for Jesus, no one would be offended, and I'd know I wasn't living the life He has required of me. I have experienced an extra measure of peace and assurance from God that all is well, because I have served and loved Him first.

Being a courageous witness for Christ also inspires others to be bold in their faith. We can actually change the dynamics of our surroundings by inviting the Lord into our conversations or situations with others. There are many times that unsaved people would like to talk about God or have prayer, but *they* fear rejection too! We can help them overcome their apprehensions by speaking up.

How Do I Share My Faith With Others?

Some people wonder how they would even begin to talk to someone about Jesus. A big part of this is to be sensitive to the Holy Spirit and to others.

1. We need to begin by being filled with His Spirit. Pray before you share with people. Ask God to put you in the right place at the right time with the right person! Many times, the Spirit will "nudge" us, by making us feel excited or nervous when He is trying to get our attention that it's time to witness.

   When we are led by the Spirit, we need to be confident that He has already prepared that person, time, and place for us already, and He will give us the right words and the adequate time we will need to share (Luke 12:11-12).
2. It is essential to be regularly immersed in His Word and in prayer, because what we "feed" on with our hearts and minds is what comes out when we talk with others. If all we hear is filthy talk from people we spend time with, or junk from the internet or television, we will be poor communicators when it comes to the Gospel message. Likewise, if we spend quality time in God's presence every day, and subject our hearts and minds to His living Sword, the Bible, we will be much more prepared.

   We need to tenderly knock on every relationship door to test its receptivity. This includes the lady at the bank and the man at the store, as well as our unsaved loved ones. LOOK for opportunities and openings in conversation. I try to be aware of phrases that people say in their everyday talk. For example, I listen for words like "My son is sick" or "I'm afraid" or "I'm not sure how to handle this situation". These are great conversations starters. In their need, they may be much more open to hearing about God.
3. We won't share our message with every single person we meet; obviously there isn't enough time for that. Indeed, we may not even

be the person God is going to use at that time. And sometimes, people just won't be open to listen. Learn to be okay with that!

4. Find a point of common interest. For example, let's say you are at the check-out counter at the store. You see that the clerk looks tired and overwhelmed. You can say something like "It seems like you're having a rough day. I feel like that sometimes in my work, as well".

   At this point, you can tell him or her that prayer really helps you when you're stressed. Or, you can say "I'll be praying for you". Remember, it takes about 1-2 minutes to check your groceries and bag them, so you really do have plenty of time to get a short message across.

   Many people have told me afterwards that the comment I shared with them during this kind of short exchange really encouraged them. Once the relationship was forged, they often begin sharing with me and have even asked me to pray for them on future occasions.

   We can do this anywhere we go, using this technique at the bank, with telemarketers, with the daycare staff, at the hospital, at work, at school… Simply anywhere we are, we can be a beacon of salt and light, life, joy, and hope for our precious Lord. And it's really fun! ☺

5. Know that you will never be perfect. You won't have a perfect Christian life, nor will you always witness perfectly. The Holy Spirit has a beautiful way of making up for our shortcomings! He can "translate" your message so that it makes sense and is beneficial to the person you are witnessing to! People have often told me I was very clear in my message, when at the time, I really felt like I was doing a terrible job!

6. It is important to make sure that your life lines up with biblical truth as much as possible. Realize that this responsibility is partly your own choices, and much of it depends on the Holy Spirit to keep you holy. There is nothing worse than a "Christian" who is known to sleep around and have a potty mouth. When this person tries to share anything about God, they are automatically disregarded, because their words don't line up with their actions. This also

includes those who gossip and complain, as well as those who are falsely proud or overly critical (Philippians 2:14-15). This does great harm to Jesus and the Gospel.

7. We need to check our motives! Unfortunately, some Christians become aggressive or argumentative while sharing. This not only annoying, but a big turnoff. They come on too strong, and for the wrong reasons. They may feel superior, or want to throw their knowledge of Scripture around. This type of person often puts others down for their beliefs or lifestyles.

   However, this is the very attitude that has turned the world away from Jesus and the church on many occasions. Most people can sense if we are genuine or not. If we're just trying to win brownie points with God by trying to convince someone about Him, or trying to show off, but we don't really care about them, they'll know it! LOVE needs to be the Prime Mover for sharing our faith.

   Additionally, we need to be aware that if we are too weak in our approach, it has the same effect - people will be turned off to Jesus in our lives, sensing that we are not sold-out for our faith. They will likely wonder why it is they should even be interested in our Lord.

8. Try practicing what you might say to someone about your faith. You can do this in front of a mirror, or with someone who loves the Lord and is a great communicator of the Gospel message. They'll probably love to share their methods for witnessing with you.

   If you would like to learn about some other practical ways to share your faith, Chapter 12 in this book is a great tool.

   It is so much more pleasant when someone shares their experiences with us with delight and joy, and their only motive is that they want us to experience it too! This is the way to communicate our faith - joyfully and modestly - with a desire that is born out of our love for God and people.

CHAPTER 9
SHARING OUR FAITH
REFLECTION

1. **What does the word *witness* mean?**

2. **Do you have trouble sharing your faith with others? Why?**

3. **Do you believe that people who reject Jesus Christ are going to a place called hell for eternity? Does that influence your decision to share your faith?**

4. **Do you believe you have a responsibility to witness to others about Jesus? Why?**

5. **Are you willing to step out of your comfort zone to learn how to share your love for Jesus with others?**

6. **How were you brought to faith in Jesus? Did someone share their faith with you? Does that affect your choice to share with others?**

CHAPTER 10

DISCERNING GOD'S WILL

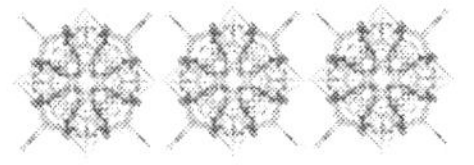

How many times have we thought "I just want to know God's will for my life. Why doesn't He just *tell* me what He wants me to do?"

Most of the Christians I have met express their desire to know God's will for their lives. The problem is, God doesn't usually speak in an audible voice. We so long to communicate with Him in our human way, and often have trouble relating to Him in the ways He has designed.

However, He has given us many ways to know His will, if we will only be open and sensitive to His leading. To "discern" means to "uncover" or "discover" or "determine" something which is not obvious. In this chapter, we'll examine some of the methods God uses to speak to us.

To begin, I believe that God intentionally leaves us with questions as to how to find Him and follow Him. This is because it requires *faith.* Indeed, Hebrews 11:1 tells us "Faith shows the reality of what we *hope for*; it is the evidence of things *we cannot see*". Hebrews 11:6 says "And it is impossible to please God **without faith**. Anyone who wants to come to Him must believe that God exists and that He rewards those who sincerely seek Him" (italics and bold mine).

If it makes you feel any better, even some of the spiritual giants in the Bible were spoken to directly by God, but they still had to go on blind faith the majority of the time.

For example, God spoke directly to Abram (God later named him Abraham) when he was living in the town of Haran. God called him to pack up his people and his things, leave his country, and go to a land that was previously unknown to Abram (Genesis 12:1). He had no idea how he was going to get there or even where the land was!

God also spoke directly to Noah, telling him to build a huge ship that would save them from a catastrophic rain storm. However, if you read up until this point in the Scriptures, "rain" hadn't even fallen before (Genesis 2:4-6). The water that was in the earth came from springs and rivers. The next time the word "rain" appears in the Bible is during the Great Flood (Genesis 7:4).

My point about both of these accounts is that God spoke directly to these men - but they had to act in faith in order to accomplish His will. God didn't draw a roadmap for Abram, and He didn't make the ship for Noah. In fact, both men would have probably been laughingstocks of their culture. To Moses: "You're going *where??* God told you *what??* To Noah: You're going to build a huge ark 7 stories high, 1 ½ football fields in length and the place is going to flood - even though we've never seen rain"?? Hahaha ☺

The truth is, our faith is increased when we don't know exactly what God is going to do next in our lives! Just as we need help navigating our way on an unfamiliar journey, we need to grasp the hand of our Lord in order for Him to help direct us to the next step into our future. Deep trust and dependency are thus developed as we cling to Jesus and follow where He leads (2 Corinthians 5:7).

Ways That God Communicates His Will To Us

There are many methods that God uses to talk to us and to let us know what He wants from us and for us. I have put together the 4 main ways: The Bible, Prayer, the Holy Spirit, and Circumstances. Under the "Bible" heading, I have listed some Scriptures that outline God's general will for all of our lives.

The Bible

Most of us would probably agree that the Bible is one of the most important and obvious ways that God reveals His will to us. He has told us everything He wants us to know through His Word. But His *specific* plan for our lives unfolds AS we obey what He has shown us in the Scriptures.

Unfortunately, a good majority of Christians in the United States do not read their Bibles regularly, and so they are ignorant of God's ways. According to a 2018 Barna study, only 14% of Americans read their Bibles daily, followed by 13% who study it 3-4 times a week. 8 percent read the Word once a week; 6 percent about once a month and 8 percent use it three to four times a year (*https://www.barna.com/research/state-of-the-bible-2018-seven-top-findings/*). I know if I read the Bible only once a month or 3-4 times a year, I would feel spiritually starved!

Some of the common reasons people don't read their Bibles are: 1. Too busy; 2. Too lazy; 3. They don't understand it; and 4. They feel convicted. But in reality, not reading our Bibles regularly is like taking a trip across country and not having a map! Without the steady hand of Scripture, we will stumble through life without purpose or direction. We desperately need the compass of Truth.

There are so many benefits to studying the Bible. We get to know God's character. We find out who we are, and why we were created. We understand where we are going, and how we should respond to our Maker and the people He fashioned.

When we read the Bible regularly, our minds are transformed, our consciences are corrected, and our hearts and spirits are strengthened. We develop a foundation upon which to build our lives. We grow in our faith, and have a rudder which will guide us in turbulent times. We realize how much we are loved. We are washed with grace and mercy, as well as convicted of our waywardness.

I wrote a chapter called "What is the Bible" in my last book, *New Beginnings: Understanding the Basic Principles of the Christian Faith.* If you're interested, you can read it for a more in-depth study about how important the Bible is and why it's essential to read it.

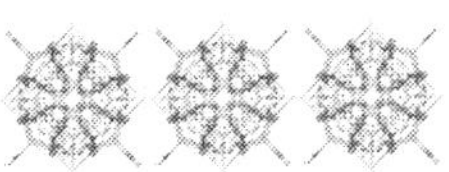

I have written out some Scriptures to help outline God's will for your lives. You can underline or highlight the verses that really speak to you:

- Deuteronomy 6:5: "And you must love the Lord your God with all your heart, all your soul, and all your strength".
- Deuteronomy 10:12-13: "And now, Israel, what does the Lord your God require of you? He requires only that you fear the Lord your God, and live in a way that pleases Him, and love Him and serve Him with all your heart and soul. And you must always obey the Lord's commands and decrees that I am giving you today for your own good". (This passage was written to the Israelites in the Old Testament, but it applies to all of God's people throughout history).
- Micah 6:8: "No, O people, the Lord has told you what is good, and this is what He requires of you: to do what is right, to love mercy, and to walk humbly with your God".
- Acts 22:14: "Then he told me, 'The God of our ancestors has chosen you to know His will and to see the Righteous One and hear Him speak'". (This verse is talking about Jesus, the Righteous One).
- Romans 12:1-2: "And so, dear brothers and sisters, I plead with you to give your bodies to God because of all He has done for you. Let them be a living and holy sacrifice - the kind He will find acceptable. This is truly the way to worship Him.

  Don't copy the behavior and customs of this world, but let God transform you into a new person by changing the way you think. Then you will learn to know God's will for you, which is good and pleasing and perfect".
- 2 Corinthians 13:11: "Dear brothers and sisters, I close my letter with these last words: Be joyful. Grow to maturity. Encourage each other. Live in harmony and peace. Then the God of love and peace will be with you".
- Ephesians 4:29-30: "Don't use foul or abusive language. Let everything you say be good and helpful, so that your words will be an encouragement to those who hear them. And do not bring sorrow to God's Holy Spirit by the way you live. Remember, He has

identified you as His own, guaranteeing that you will be saved on the day of redemption".

- Colossians 1:9-12: "So we have not stopped praying for you since we first heard about you. We ask God to give you complete knowledge of His will and to give you spiritual wisdom and understanding. Then the way you live will always honor and please the Lord, and your lives will produce every kind of good fruit.

  All the while, you will grow as you learn to know God better and better. We also pray that you will be strengthened with all His glorious power so you will have all the endurance and patience you need. May you be filled with joy, always thanking the Father. He has enabled you to share in the inheritance that belongs to His people, who live in the light".
- Colossians 4:2: "Devote yourselves to prayer with an alert mind and a thankful heart".
- 1 Thessalonians 4:3-5: "God's will is for you to be holy, so stay away from all sexual sin. Then each of you will control his own body and live in holiness and honor; not in lustful passion like the pagans who do not know God and His ways".
- 1 Thessalonians 5:10-25: "Christ died for us so that, whether we are dead or alive when He returns, we can live with Him forever. So encourage each other and build each other up, just as you are already doing.

  Dear brothers and sisters, honor those who are your leaders in the Lord's work. They work hard among you and give you spiritual guidance. Show them great respect and wholehearted love because of their work. And live peacefully with each other.

  Brothers and sisters, we urge you to warn those who are lazy. Encourage those who are timid. Take tender care of those who are weak. Be patient with everyone. See that no one pays back evil for evil, but always try to do good to each other and to all people. Always be joyful. Never stop praying. Be thankful in all circumstances, for this is God's will for you who belong to Christ Jesus.

Do not stifle the Holy Spirit. Do not scoff at prophecies, but test everything that is said. Hold on to what is good. Stay away from every kind of evil. Now may the God of peace make you holy in every way, and may your whole spirit and soul and body be kept blameless until our Lord Jesus Christ comes again. God will make this happen, for He who calls you is faithful. Dear brothers and sisters, pray for us".

- Hebrews 10:10: "For God's will was for us to be made holy by the sacrifice of the body of Jesus Christ, once for all time".

Prayer

We probably all realize that prayer is another way we communicate with God. But ironically, it's another discipline that is often overlooked or ignored! Christians actually pray more than they read the Bible, but still, according to a Pew study from 2016, only half of American Christians pray daily and feel that God hears them and answers their prayers (*https://www.pewresearch.org/fact-tank/2016/05/04/5-facts-about-prayer*). Of course, more than half of Christians pray, but they do so with less consistency or faith that they'll be heard.

The Bible tells us to pray at all times (Ephesians 6:18; 1 Thessalonians 5:17). This may seem a bit unreasonable, but we really can be in prayer constantly throughout the day. I pray for people I come in contact with all the time. Even when I walk by someone and don't speak to them, I try to look at their face and see how they might be feeling. If I see someone who looks sad or angry, I immediately lift them up to the Lord in prayer.

My husband and I try to start every morning with prayer and Bible study. This helps ground us and it brings new light and direction to our day. Now I don't pretend to be super spiritual, so don't get me wrong. I'm just saying that these are ways that I keep myself close to God - because I need Him SO desperately, and I know my life would be a complete wreck without Him!

Prayer is actually a way of releasing our fears and concerns, and giving them over to the Lord. We may have to do this many times a day! Prayer also helps us to "get out of ourselves" and think of others who are going through worse troubles.

God will definitely talk to you during your prayer time. You can tell Him what's on your mind, and then take some quiet time to just *listen* to what He might want to say to you. Also, if we are praying according to *God's* will, He can answer our prayers more readily, because we have HIS mind and heart in the matter (1 John 5:14-15).

Another way to work through your prayer time is to write down your thoughts and prayer requests (journaling) in a notebook or on a computer. I personally don't journal, but my husband Michael wanted to share what has helped him *so much*. This is what he wrote:

"Journaling is simply writing out your concerns, or problems that you need God's help and wisdom to resolve. I really like using a tablet and you will see why later. I start out by thinking about and defining *exactly* what my problem is. *Then, I write it out* onto a page, which takes time and thought. It requires that you "name your concern" and are able to define it, write it out, and get it OUT of you onto paper! I find just getting it on paper helps a lot; but then right below the *pages of woes* and concerns, I will write out a prayer giving "all of the above" to God.

Here is where it gets real interesting. See, not only does writing it out make you focus, it SLOWS you down. I start my prayer by asking for forgiveness of my sins, that nothing would hinder me from drawing near to God. I ask Him to slow me down, and clear the clutter from my mind so I can sense his Spirit, His will, and His replies to my questions. As I am writing out the prayer to God, I remain *vigilant* to "hear something that God may want to say to me". I pause....after writing my question or issue to Him, *and listen* for what comes into my mind. When I do hear something from Him, "***I will write down what I hear***" in quotation marks. That way, if I read over a prayer from long ago, I will know that I felt *"that"* was from the Lord! Of course, I test "what I hear" against what the Bible says, as God will never contradict His Word. I am fully aware that our enemy would love to deceive and trap me. But so often, what I hear is exactly what I needed to know or to do!

After journaling, then praying, I go to the very back page of the tablet and write the date with my specific prayer request(s) that I am searching for answers to, or sometimes, "what I heard" Him tell me to do. I leave some extra writing space under each shortened prayer request for when God answers that prayer, or for when the issue is resolved. I return to the Journal to write out how each prayer was resolved and the date when it happened. *In due time*, seeing all of the ***answered prayers*** is ASTOUNDING to witness! It also gives me a "testimony" to share with others who may be going through trials themselves. It confirms that God is hearing me and dealing with the issues I have asked Him to help me with.

I have found that sometimes God's answer can be "yes", "wait", "maybe", "later", or "no" so I never want to rush ahead of His leading. And often times "waiting upon the Lord" can be the best, yet hardest thing to do! Our trials are all to build and mold us into His image. Waiting on God builds our faith and trust. Running to Jesus through Journaling is a great way to try to "discern His will" and witness it in action! I hope this helps someone as much as it has helped me! (Do keep that journal in a safe place from any prying eyes!)

This brings us to the third way God speaks to us: through His Holy Spirit.

The Holy Spirit

It takes time and effort to learn how to hear from God's Spirit. Just as it is in a new relationship, we don't automatically "know" what the other person likes or thinks, or what they believe. As we read the Bible and pray, we will learn what God thinks and desires. He often speaks to us through His Spirit (1 Corinthians 2:10-16).

Since we have the Holy Spirit living inside of us, we already have an advantage. But He won't yell at us! We can stifle His voice, which the Bible calls "A still, small voice; a gentle whisper". He speaks to our hearts, but if we are too busy to listen, we will fail to hear Him. We must be willing to shut out the noise of the world and ask for His input.

In our world of chaos, this is a difficult lesson to learn. The Holy Spirit loves to impart wisdom to us. His job is to guide us, fill us, teach us truth, and empower us. In fact, God will give us the power and the desire we need to do His will (Philippians 2:13). But we need to cultivate an intimate relationship with His Spirit in order to live a dynamic Christian life!

Some practical ways to obtain power and direction from the Holy Spirit are to turn off the electronics we constantly use. If possible, find a place where you can be alone. And even if you can't be completely alone, you can train your mind to concentrate on Jesus. I have done this myself, when it was impossible to find solitude. God will meet you where you are.

Circumstances

How many times have we seen people flock to church or begin to pray after something devastating has happened in their lives? The death of a loved one; a catastrophic natural disaster; a life-threatening illness...

Oftentimes, people *blame* God through these hard times. What we need to realize is that God isn't always the one who causes our circumstances. At times it's our own bad choices. Sometimes it's the devil stirring up havoc. And other times, difficulty comes just by living in a sin-sick, fallen world.

Additionally, there are times when God *will* back us into a corner to get our attention. But no matter who is behind our circumstances or why we face adversity, God can use these times to bring us closer to Himself, and to get us to see what is truly important in our lives (Genesis 50:20).

Finally, we always have the free will to deny the Lord or to disobey Him. But the consequences aren't worth it in the end (Romans 1:24-32). When we refuse His ways, we just won't have the satisfaction in life that we're craving. Doing His will brings us immeasurable and eternal benefit (Romans 2:7). If we take the time to learn from our hardships; if we allow God to strengthen us and sharpen us through them; and if we use these opportunities to grow closer to Him, we'll be able to determine His will and hear His voice more clearly. This will always benefit us.

Besides, being led by the Lord to discover His plan every day is so exciting! You never know what He has in store for you! We are only truly fulfilled when we are living in the center of God's will. Even Jesus' nourishment was to do His Father's will, and it is no different with us as His followers (John 4:34; 6:38). And as we follow His lead, we'll be nourished so that we will be able to "water and feed" other people spiritually. The harvest is human souls for eternity.

Wow!

CHAPTER 10
DISCERNING GOD'S WILL
REFLECTION

1. **What are 4 things you have learned about God's will for your life? "I now know God wants me to:**

    ____

    ____

    ____

    ____

2. **What are 4 common ways that God communicates His will to us?**

    ____

    ____

    ____

    ____

3. **What are 2 ways you can change your lifestyle so you'll have more time and energy to hear from the Lord?**

    ____

    ____

4. **Do you believe that God has a specific plan for your life? From your experiences with Him, where do you think He is trying to direct you at this time?**

    ____

    ____

    ____

5. **Are you willing to follow His lead, or are you convinced that *your* plans will work?**

6. **Do you read the Bible and pray regularly? Why or why not?**

7. **Do you believe this is an essential part of your relationship with God?**

8. **Are you willing to set time aside in your day (possibly when you're most energetic) to spend this time with God?**

CHAPTER 11

THE VICTORIOUS LIFE

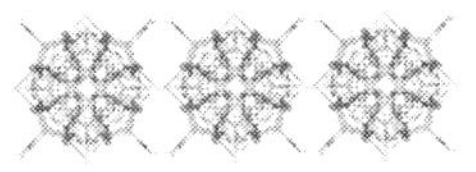

One more day. One more bill. One more fight with my spouse. One more workout at the gym. Onc more day of work. One more worry. One more exam. One more health problem. And the list goes on.

Does it ever seem to you that life is only a series of struggles? Is it ever hard for you to just get up in the morning and face another day of monotony? Do you ever feel hopeless, wondering if you are making a difference in this world? Do you lack peace and joy?

If you are a Christian, this is not the life that God has planned for you. He saved you so you can live in *overcoming victory*!

We Already Are the Victors!

Colossians 1:15-20 is a description of the Lord Jesus Christ. He is our God and King! He has already gone before us and won the battle. He is powerful and capable. Our Leader is trustworthy and truthful (Ephesians 3:20).

Romans 8:15-39 tells us how abundantly we are blessed! We have a Father who loves us unconditionally and forever. The devil will not win over our lives (even though we may feel defeated at times). We will eventually share in God's glory.

Nothing can separate us from Jesus if we truly love Him (John 10:29). As Christians, no one can condemn us (Romans 8:1), because Jesus took our payment on the cross. Death is only the beginning of the most magnificent experience we can even imagine (1 Corinthians 2:9). We have heaven to look forward to.

Tools to Help You Overcome

Do you have sort of a 'head knowledge' that God's promises are true, but you don't believe they're really for you? Are you failing to live as if you are REAL royalty? Are you living like a pauper, or like an expectant, beloved child who will inherit all the riches of heaven and earth from your Daddy (Ephesians 1:3-4, 11-20)?

Ephesians 2:4-10 talks about how precious we are to the Lord, and that He has given us an inheritance because of that love. If we are continually complaining, worrying, and wringing our hands with negative attitudes and downcast spirits - fear and self-centeredness - then what in the world are we showing those who don't know Him?

2 Corinthians 10:3-5 tells us that the "weapons" we use as Christians are not human instruments. In other words, we are in a spiritual battle. We must use God's tools to fight - to overcome - and not our own. Satan laughs in the face of believers who try to fight in the flesh! We are no match for his crafty ways. Only God can equip us for this war.

God's Word states that we are children of the Triune Godhead - the Father, Son and Holy Spirit. So our status as royalty is revealed. We belong to the family of God - He is the Omnipotent (All-Powerful), Omnipresent (Everywhere at once), and Omniscient (All-Knowing) Creator. So our position in the Kingdom is real.

And we are the Bride of Christ, Who is our Rightful King. Our victory is already established, and our heavenly place secure. Choosing to believe these truths will change our hearts, minds, and attitudes. It will give us the power we need to be victorious. God wants us to know we are each His masterpiece. He created us so we could do the good things He already planned for us (Ephesians 2:10).

Remember, before we received Jesus, we were always free to sin, but now we are free to *choose* holy living (Galatians 5:16). And now, we are FREE to think God's thoughts. It's a choice (Philippians 4:6-9). This way of believing doesn't mean we put our head in the sand and pretend there aren't problems or suffering in the world.

But it does mean that we direct our thoughts towards the Lord in *every* situation. Make Him your first go-to Guy! When a negative thought comes in – TAKE IT CAPTIVE! If it doesn't line up with the Word of God, then **toss it out!**

For example, if your negative inner voice says "You're just not as attractive, thin, rich, educated, etc., as another person", then replace the thought with "God made me uniquely. He has given me gifts, talents, looks, and abilities like NO ONE ELSE in this world!"

If you hear "There's no hope. This problem, situation, person, etc., will never change". Replace it with "My God is a God of impossibilities. I will walk towards Him in faith that He will show me the next step. He will give me the necessary power and insight that I need. As I delight myself in Him, I will not lean on my own understanding, but will acknowledge Him in ALL of my ways" (Proverbs 3:5-6).

You see, replacing our old thought patterns with what God's Word says gives us the POWER to overcome. Our God is a forward-thinking, positive, and miraculous God. Our destination is heaven, so at the very least, we can set our focus there and remember that our life is but a breath - it will end before we know it (James 4:14).

What's more exciting is that the best is yet to come! The pain we are feeling, the troubles we have, and the situation we are in WILL CHANGE (Romans 8:18, 23; 1 Corinthians 15:43; 2 Corinthians 4:17). It's a promise from God Himself.

If you have no control over a situation, then GIVE IT TO GOD. Worrying about our present situation or our future will not change it. This will just disable us from acting when the future arrives - when it becomes 'today'.

And if you *do* have control over a situation, pray about your response before you act. Ask Him if this is a situation you *should* be doing something about. Ask Him for power, wisdom, and direction. Then, do everything you can by the Spirit's power and to the glory of God! You'll need God's guidance no matter what your circumstances are.

God's ultimate game plan is to bring everything and everyone under His authority in heaven and on earth (Ephesians 1:9-11). He is in complete control of the universe, even as humans run to and fro and try to ruin God's grand design.

We can live by this old adage:

God, grant me the serenity to accept the things I cannot change,
the courage to change the things I can,
and the wisdom to know the difference.

Our God is a Victorious God and WE ARE HIS!

Here are a few Scriptures that will uplift your spirits. As I've said plenty of times in this book, we need to wrap our minds around God's truth. We must choose to discard the lies we might have been raised with, and those we still may carry with us. When our minds are transformed by His Word, we will be able to live in victory. I will highlight the beautiful nuggets in the passages below these Scripture verses:

Psalm 48:9-10

"O God, we meditate on Your unfailing love as we worship in Your Temple. As Your name deserves, O God, You will be praised to the ends of the earth. Your strong right hand is filled with victory".

Meditate on His unchanging love for us
Worship Him because He is worthy and deserves our praise
He is "filled" with victory, so with Him, we can be assured of triumph in our lives

Psalm 62:1-2

"I wait quietly before God, for my victory comes from Him. He alone is my rock and my salvation, my fortress where I will never be shaken".

Wait on the Lord. Sit in His presence and let Him minister to you
Our victory comes only from God
He is a true Rock, one that cannot be shaken by circumstances
He is our salvation. We have been saved from eternal doom!
God is our fortress. We can "hide in Him" for protection and stability

Psalm 98:1-3

"Sing a new song to the Lord, for He has done wonderful deeds. His right hand has won a mighty victory; His holy arm has shown His saving power! The Lord has announced His victory and has revealed His righteousness to every nation! He has remembered His promise to love and be faithful

to Israel (This also applies to those who have received Jesus as Savior - His people). *The ends of the earth have seen the victory of our God".*

Sing to the Lord. This is a great way to change our focus!

Think about the wonderful things He's done - family, friends, nature, love....

He has already won our victory because He has the power we need

He is righteous, which means He is right in all He says and does

He has not forgotten His promises to love and be faithful to His people

Isaiah 12

"In that day you will sing: 'I will praise you, O Lord! You were angry with me, but not anymore. Now you comfort me. See, God has come to save me. I will trust in Him and not be afraid. The Lord God is my strength and my song; He has given me victory.' With joy you will drink deeply from the fountain of salvation! In that wonderful day you will sing: "Thank the Lord! Praise His name! Tell the nations what He has done. Let them know how mighty He is! Sing to the Lord, for He has done wonderful things. Make known His praise around the world. Let all the people of Jerusalem shout His praise with joy! For great is the Holy One of Israel who lives among you".

God is our God of comfort. Let Him comfort you!

He is our Savior and completely trustworthy. Don't be afraid!

God is our strength. We are not weak with Him by our side

God is our Joy. Lift up your face and smile about that!

Tell others about Jesus - it will brighten your day ☺

God is mighty and able. He is wonderful and powerful.

God lives inside of you by His Holy Spirit. That is amazing!

Isaiah 52:10

"The Lord has demonstrated His holy power before the eyes of all the nations. All the ends of the earth will see the victory of our God"

One day, everyone will see God as He really is. We will all bow before Him, whether in love or in fear (Philippians 2:9-11). We will see His glory. We will spend eternity in Heaven loving God - or in Hell separated from Him and all goodness. It is our choice.

Romans 8:37
"No, despite all these things, overwhelming victory is ours through Christ, who loved us"
We're not just overcomers, we are super-conquerors!
1 Corinthians 15: 54-58
"Then, when our dying bodies have been transformed into bodies that will never die, this Scripture will be fulfilled: "Death is swallowed up in victory. O death, where is your victory? O death, where is your sting?" For sin is the sting that results in death, and the law gives sin its power. But thank God! He gives us victory over sin and death through our Lord Jesus Christ. So, my dear brothers and sisters, be strong and immovable. Always work enthusiastically for the Lord, for you know that nothing you do for the Lord is ever useless"
Our bodies will be changed eternally and perfectly
We no longer have to be afraid of death when we receive salvation
God has already given us victory over powerful spiritual forces
We can be strong and not moved by circumstances
We have real purpose in this life, and the privilege of working for the Lord
Nothing we do for Him is ever wasted
We will reap eternal rewards

So, do you see from these amazing Scriptures that we don't have to be depressed or fearful?? ☺

I encourage you to read similar passages in the Bible for yourself. What do you think God is trying to say to you?

Believe God's Word About Your Ability to Overcome

Here's a way to focus your mind on God's truth about your life in Christ. You can read it daily to train your mind to believe God's Word:

I choose to walk in the Position that Jesus Christ has put me. I am nothing in myself - that much is true. But according to the salvation of my Lord - the Majestic Authority, I am elevated to a level of great honor and privilege in the Household of God. And I will hold my head high so that I represent my Royal Family in gratitude and grace.

I will choose to believe what God has spoken to me through His Spirit and His Word. I will decidedly and forcefully throw out every thought that does not line up with what God says is true about me, my situation, and my future. I will bring all thoughts of hopelessness, self absorption, and self-condemnation to a halt when it enters my mind and replace it with God's Truth.

And I will live out the values I profess by putting Jesus Christ first in my life. I know this will entail a sacrifice of my time, energy, and resources, but I know that the outcome will be an eternal tree of luscious fruit. I will give up a portion of my morning sleep or routine to meet with God in prayer and to study the Bible.

In order to make this a part of my life, I make a promise this very day to ask the Lord for *the desire* to meet with Him daily and intimately. If I need to stop an extra activity I am involved in that is not necessary or relevant to my walk with Christ, I will choose to refrain from it. I will choose to stop a portion of my television, internet and/or social media use in order to spend time with God. I will determine *whatever it is* that is keeping me from quality time with Him and ask His Spirit to help me change.

More Amazing Benefits to Overcoming

We have already read so many Scriptures about how privileged we are in Christ. We have an abundance of treasures, both now and forever because we know the Living God. But I would like to list the final gems that Jesus Himself told us we would possess as overcomers in His Kingdom:

- Revelation 2:7
- Revelation 2:11
- Revelation 2:17
- Revelation 2: 19
- Revelation 2: 26
- Revelation 3:5
- Revelation 3:12
- Revelation 3:21
- Revelation 15:2

- Revelation 21:7

We have an indescribable joy that awaits us if we overcome!

Lord, I pray right now for the strength to step out of my comfort zone and to move into the life You have already set in motion for me before the foundation of the world. There are things I know I should be doing, but have failed to do.

There are also negative and harmful areas in my thoughts, attitudes and actions that I cannot see clearly, and I ask You to show them to me in the upcoming days, weeks and months.

I pray fervently for the desire to overcome my fleshly way of thinking. I beseech You today for great power from Your Precious Holy Spirit to replace my old attitudes and mindsets. I want my life to change into a life that mirrors the sacrificial purposes of Jesus Christ, and that exhibits the fruit of Your Spirit, clearly and passionately. Amen

If we are basking in His presence and echoing His glory
from our lives, we are promised a victorious life!

CHAPTER 11
THE VICTORIOUS LIFE
REFLECTION

1. **Do you feel you are living a life of victory with Jesus right now? Why or why not?**

2. **Do you believe that God wants you to be victorious? Do you doubt His power to lead you into a life of victory? If so, why?**

3. **What are some of the "Victory" Scriptures listed in this chapter that really touched your heart/mind/spirit?**

4. **Using the Scriptures you listed in #3, would you be willing to spend some time each day to read them again? (This will help to transform your thinking, which can then change your beliefs and attitudes about your situation (Romans 12:2).**

____

____

____

____

____

5. **What are some of the obstacles in your life that are keeping you from victory?**

____

____

____

____

____

6. **What does it mean to *you* to live in victory?**

____

____

____

____

____

CHAPTER 12

THE FOUR LEGGED CHURCH

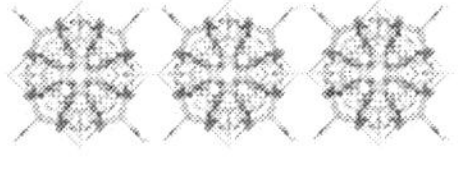

What in the world is a four legged church?
Why, it's a church with four legs, of course! ☺
This church is stable, healthy, and well-balanced

While this subject may not pertain directly to discipleship, this book would have been incomplete without mentioning the importance of finding a biblically solid church.

There are thousands of churches in the world, and I believe God, in His creative wisdom, brings *most* of them together under His umbrella of "The Church". (I say "most of them" because some churches are simply not following the guidelines of Christ or His Word).

The beauty of the Church is that regardless of where you live, what nationality you are, or which culture you live in, if you believe in Jesus Christ, and love Him and serve Him with your life, you are part of His collective Church (Ephesians 3:6).

That being said, as you have probably gathered throughout this book, I feel there is a serious lack of true discipleship in the American Body of Christ. I cannot attest to other countries, as I have not attended services outside of the United States. But I have read scores of reports and stories of people in other countries who risk their lives to obtain just one page of Scripture, or of walking miles just to be with other believers.

In my opinion, part of the problem in the United States is that we are a spoiled and wealthy country. This isn't a new issue, though. All throughout the Old Testament, when Israel had come to a place where they had "all they wanted", they became *self-sufficient* and moved away from God.

Another hindrance to people coming to Jesus in America is that they have been saturated with the Gospel so much, and many have rejected the message so often, that their hearts are hardened towards Christ's love and offer of salvation. Even Christians have trouble staying true to their Lord at times; indeed, the Bible talks about a "great falling away" of the Church in the last days (2 Timothy 3:1-5).

And last, but not least, another difficulty lies in the fact that many preachers are reluctant to share the Gospel in its entirety. God's grace is highlighted so heavily that it has become distorted - sort of like a vending machine mentality: "If you accept Jesus, you won't have to worry about your life again! He'll give you everything you want just by praying and believing hard enough! He wants you to be happy, carefree, and wealthy"!

Some pastors won't even mention the word "sin" or "dying to self" or "hell" in their sermons. Worse, they don't even believe in these biblical concepts! They think preaching on these topics "shames" their parishioners, and that they will turn away from God. Or they worry that people won't want to come to their church if they are confronted with their transgressions. And there are times when church members who tithe generously have more control over the church than the leadership.

It seems that the days when we were taught to be disciplined in our faith - such as reading the Word of God regularly, tithing, fasting, praying without ceasing, and going out of our four walls to reach the lost - are lost. Programs and church buildings have become more important than people. Money, prestige, and entertainment have outweighed humility and self-sacrifice.

While this is certainly not true of every church, my husband and I have found this phenomena to be ever-increasing. As a result of our ministry and traveling, we have visited so many churches that we've lost count.

While we've found that nearly every church had *something* good about it, when we inquired about discipleship classes, New Believer classes, or Christian outreach in their communities, many churches were sorely lacking.

It's true we haven't actually gone back to these churches to see how they operate on a regular basis, and although we're certainly not experts on critiquing this problem, we ran across these common themes so often that we began to ask ourselves: "What do *we* think would be the most impactful kind of church? What would be some practical measures we could use if we were to look for a church"?

Which Church Should I Attend?

As Christians, our first and foremost responsibility is our own personal relationship with Christ. A church body is only as healthy as its individual members. We have already read about cultivating a deep, loving, steadfast, and healthy connection with the Lord in previous chapters. Everything else in our life springs from this foundation.

So to begin with, we need to find a wholesome, nourishing and dynamic church to attend. This is harder than it sounds. This isn't just about finding a place where we feel comfortable, although that is an important aspect. A good place to begin is to pray about the place where GOD wants us to call our church home.

This is probably a good time to mention that if you're in a church that is putting you to sleep, or is just a social club, you may want to pray about finding a church that stimulates you to grow, and also teaches you to share your faith.

That being said, I do NOT believe in "church hopping" - that is, going from church to church in search of the "perfect" place, or leaving a church because one person hurt your feelings or you don't like the color of the carpet! Being part of a church often means going through rough patches as well as good seasons, just like any normal relationship. Just be sensitive to the Lord's leading.

If you are part of a church that doesn't seem very healthy, but you feel God wants you to stay there, then start praying for the congregants and the leadership. You can even invite others to join you in a small prayer meeting. This does wonders for yourselves, as well as for the church!

Another important aspect of keeping our faith alive is to attend a small group Bible study. As I've said, there should be classes available for new believers and discipleship in your church. The leaders of these groups should know the Word of God well and have a passion for teaching. This leader should stimulate you to grow and to want to change into Christ's likeness. And if there are no classes like these, maybe God will use *you* to start one! ☺

What are the "Four Legs"?

If you think about a stool with four legs, you'll realize that each "leg" needs to be equal in length. Every leg needs to be strong and able to handle the weight of the person sitting on it. If one leg is weak or damaged, the stool as a whole will be ineffective – and could even be dangerous.

The first leg of a healthy church is *biblical preaching.* Determining if our church is healthy is difficult. We don't want to be overly critical, but at the same time, we don't want to ignore potential dangers to our faith.

Again, messages from the pastor should include God's loving side, as well as His character trait of justice. Without balancing these two aspects of God's personality, we get a lop-sided view of what He offers us - as well as what He expects of us. We need to hear that His grace is overwhelming and far-reaching, but we also need to be taught that our sin has consequences and He will not tolerate a lukewarm effort from us.

I have been to churches where the emphasis is on how much God wants to bless me. While it's true that God wants the best for me, there was no mention of my responsibility to the relationship.

At another church I attended, the pastor spent half of the message on how much money his congregation was to give (and this was a weekly practice according to several of the congregants). The leadership actually sat at the front of the church during the offering to watch how much was being put into their huge **buckets**!!

My husband and I went to another church where the pastor was *yelling* at his flock about their sin and how "bad" they were. We left the service before it was over.

There were still others churches where people were walking around and speaking in tongues so loudly that I was unable to focus on praying for the church before the service, or on the pastor's message during the service.

In my experience, none of these churches had the feel of the Holy Spirit in them. If you're interested in learning more about the Holy Spirit, there's a chapter about this in my *New Beginnings* book.

Again, we shouldn't become overly critical or judgmental. However, I have found that many people just "go to church" without really knowing who their pastor is or what he believes. They don't have a clue as to what their church's mission statement is, how they feel about giving, or what their church does for community or world outreach.

I think it's a good idea to meet with the pastor (whether you have been at the church for some time or you are new) and ask some important questions. Some of them might include:

What do you believe about sin?
What do you believe about hell?
Do you believe that the Holy Bible is absolute truth?
Do you believe that I have responsibilities to God?

You might want to brush up on your own beliefs about these issues even before you visit with the leadership of your church. Knowing what you believe helps you to gauge if you are in the right place. And be willing to hear differing views - you may be off in your own theology and the pastor is correct in his.

The Second Leg

The second part of a healthy church is worshipful worship. Music is one of the best ways for our hearts, minds, and spirits to connect with the Lord. In fact, God instituted musical worship way back in the Old Testament. Sometimes, it was a pretty rowdy affair (Psalm 81:2; 150:4)!

You might feel uncomfortable with real worship. It's not just about singers and instrumentalists, soundboards, and mouthing words on a page. You may shy away from the emotions that accompany this form of adoration of God. But He wants so much more from us! He wants our entire being to be connected to Him. And music is one of the most powerful ways He has designed for us to worship Him.

I have often been overwhelmed by His Spirit through music, as He draws my heart into His presence. And it *is* a little unsettling at times! He is so deep and I almost feel a loss of control when I exalt the Living God! Now, this doesn't mean rolling around on the floor or screaming out!

I'm talking about having my feelings flooded with love, awe, reverence, and deep gratitude for my Lord. It can be a little intimidating to experience this, but it is so refreshing, so vital to my Christian walk. Worship through music fills my spirit, my heart, and my soul in ways I cannot obtain from any other method.

Do you feel drawn closer to God as a result of the worship music at your church? Is there time to reflect on the beauty of Christ during the worship, or are they rushing to get through the songs so they can get to the next "order of business" in the service?

Think about the way you sing to God during this time. If you are just singing the words or tapping your foot to the rhythm with no emotion, you may be missing out one of the most intimate, fulfilling means of connecting with God.

One of the best experiences we've had in a worship service was when we were speaking in a prison setting with over 200 men. My husband and I were in the front row, and when we looked in back of us, we saw scores of men weeping and raising their hands in worship. You could tell they *knew* what God had done for them and they were affected deeply. *That's* true adoration and worship!

Perhaps you might consider speaking to your music leader or pastor and find out if they might consider more worshipful music. Or, you can visit another church that may offer this kind of experience during the week, while still attending your own church on Sunday. You might find you really enjoy letting your heart and spirit soar!

The Third Leg

The third leg of a healthy church is outreach. We have spoken to many Christians who do "nice" things for people; even so far as going on short mission trips overseas. But when asked if they shared the Gospel during their journey, we've heard "No, we only helped dig wells". Or, "No, we helped build a house".

Now helping people with practical needs is great! In fact, it should be the "platform" we use as an opportunity to share the Gospel. But for the church to go out and perform only humanitarian acts without sharing their faith is negligent! The only group of people that will share Christ is Christians, and that should be our *top priority* (Matthew 28:18-20)!

Outreach can take many forms. Some ways that my husband and I share the Gospel are to buy someone in need a meal. We ask them their name and how they're doing, and offer to pray for them. We talk to them about the Lord and ask what they believe about Jesus. Oftentimes, we'll leave them with one of my books or a Bible so they have something to read and remember our conversation with.

Another way we do outreach is we've had a sign made up that says "May we pray for you"? On the sign is an offer of free books and Bibles. We have been to disaster areas, beaches, and promenades and had amazing results! People have come to Christ, and we've been able to pray with many people.

When we go out to eat, we'll chat with the waiter and *purposefully look* for an opportunity to share the Lord, invite them to church, or make ourselves available if they have any further questions. While we don't do this with every person we meet, we try to keep our "antennae" up to see if the Holy Spirit has someone for us to witness to.

We've also had thousands of outreach brochures printed up with the Gospel message in them. We leave them with waiters, on park benches, rest stops, Post Offices, bulletin boards, Laundromats, and just about everywhere we go. We had a lady come to the Lord that way. They are simply seeds that are planted for the Lord to use, and we pray that just the right person will find them!

My husband hands these brochures out at car shows, farmers markets, holiday events and anywhere else people congregate in large numbers. He simply asks people "Would you like a brochure?" Almost everyone he asks accepts the brochure. Also, it's a great conversation starter, or even just a way to leave them with something to think about.

If your church has no outreach, you can begin doing it yourself. Pray about what God might want you to do. Be creative! The point is to be *outwardly* focused. Just having a little club at church is not what Jesus had in mind when He built His Church! In fact, if Jesus' followers had stayed within their own church and circle of friends, we probably wouldn't have the Church today!

- If you are interested in using any of our material for outreach, please contact us (Be Transformed Ministries contact information is listed in the front of this book). We can send you these tools at 20% above cost.
- For more ideas, you can watch our 2 minute ministry YouTube video at *https://www.facebook.com/betransformedministries/videos/267549847281329/*
- You can also go to our ministry Facebook page to see other ways we reach out to the lost at facebook.com/betransformedministries

Please understand that I am NOT trying to promote my books or ministry. I am trying to give you some tools and ideas to work with so you can go out and begin doing the great Commission!

The Fourth Leg

The fourth important leg of the church is *fellowship*. In the Bible, the Greek word used for fellowship is "Koinonia" (coin-o-knee-ya), which simply means a group of believers gathering together to share a common bond. Of course, our bond is Jesus Christ. The New Testament believers met together regularly (Acts 2:42), and this is the pattern we are to follow.

God designed His Church as one of the most important ways to help Christians grow and receive support as we live in this world that is often contrary to His ways. It's important to note that the church is made up of people, not a building; so it's a growing (or dying) organism. (However, that doesn't mean an online church takes the place of meeting in person)...

We were created to be in relationship, so coming together to be built up in our most holy faith is essential (Jude 1:20-21). We are not supposed to be lone rangers. Whenever I hear someone say "I don't need to go to church to be a Christian", or "It's not necessary for me to attend church to practice my faith", red flags appear in my mind. While it's not about the building, per se, it *is* about the supernatural interaction of His people that brings such benefit.

The Bible tells us that "iron sharpens iron", which means that we need each other to keep us from drifting off into our own thinking (Proverbs 27:17). We need to hear the Word of God preached and taught. We need to worship together, because the Body of Christ is not made up of just a "finger or a foot" - it's a complete unit - a body - that is at its best when it is properly fit together (1Corinthians 12:12-27; Ephesians 4:16).

Additionally, there are those who are more mature in their faith, and they can help the less mature or weaker believers navigate the way. Conversely, there are others who may be more established in certain areas in their faith, and can help someone else grow in Christ.

I hope you are fortunate enough to be able to find a home church where you're welcomed, needed, and called for service.

I pray that you have learned much from this book. I hope it is a tool you will refer to often to continue helping you become a Dynamic Disciple of Jesus Christ.

CHAPTER 12
THE FOUR LEGGED CHURCH
REFLECTION

1. **Are you excited to go to your church every week? Why or why not?**

   ____

   ____

2. **Do you feel you are growing in your faith as a result of your pastor's teaching?**

   ____

   ____

3. **Are you involved in a small group Bible study? Why or why not?**

   ____

   ____

   ____

4. **Is your church gathering or small group stimulating you to action, or is it more of a "social club"?**

   ____

   ____

   ____

5. **Do you feel God's Spirit when you are worshiping through music? Or do you feel "dry" when you are singing praise songs?**

   ____

   ____

   ____

6. **From what you've learned in this study, what do you now think of Christian "outreach"?**

7. **Would you be willing to use some of the ideas in this book to begin doing your own outreach? Or even think of some of your own ways to reach people for Jesus?**

May the Lord bless you and keep you; May His face shine upon you and may He be gracious to you. May the Lord show you His favor and give you peace.

Numbers 6:24-26

Made in the USA
Columbia, SC
30 June 2021